CW01023937

Endorsem

"I tell you the truth, anyone who has faith in me will do what I have been doing. He will do even greater things than these." Jesus's words are an open invitation to trust Him and discover a Spirit-led life, a Spirit-breathed life, a life of seeing where the Father moves and moving with Him. And it ought to fill every child of God with a sense of destiny. There is a difference between making a living and making a life. So many people settle for the former. God invites and calls us to the latter. I believe this book Jason has written will help you lay claim to the abundant life Jesus promised.

—MARK BATTERSON
Author, *The Circle Maker*
Pastor, National Community Church
Washington DC

Jason Clark writes with the same passion and authenticity that he speaks. His message is a honed spearhead piercing into the mists of our confusion and disillusion and carving a doorway for the light of God's love and truth to come streaming through. The message he is carrying is cutting-edge fresh and yet contemporaneous to the era of the first disciples. Jason has the ability to reach back into history and forward into possibility at the same moment. I highly recommend you read this book and take the opportunity to re-awaken your own sense of awe by peering into the heart of a true believer.

—JENNY SHARKEY
Author, *Christian Discipleship Book*
Director of Jesus Hub
Auckland, New Zealand

Jason is able to bring the strength of combining powerful teaching with honest, authentic, moving stories from his own life. I found myself inspired to look inside, dream, and risk total surrender to a good and faithful God.

—JARED NEUSCH
Pastor, Bethel Church
Redding, CA

I loved this book. Jason's writing carries a great combination of deep wisdom couched in wry humor. He gives clarity and insight into much of the current church culture that focuses on creating a safe place for a "tamed" people, when truthfully our satisfaction and joy in being a Christian can only come as we live in and for the story Jesus calls us to, however unorthodox that may be. The outworking of His story in our story will change the world. He calls for a people who will faithfully surrender their hearts to the revolutionary God whose name is Jesus.

Untamed is beautifully insightful, written with transparent authenticity. No hype here, nor spiritual overdrive. Here is a book that determines to show God on the ground, where the real people are. Keep swimming upstream. That's where the best life is.

—BEV MURRILL
Author, *Speak Life...and Shut the Hell Up!,*
Catalysts, and *You Can Be God's Agent for Change*
Newcastle, Australia
www.bevmurrill.com

If you've died a few deaths or tasted resurrection once or twice, you're going to find yourself hidden somewhere in these pages. Jason delivers another book full of rich storytelling and life-giving reflection. You might find again who you are called to be, and forget what you are going through.

I was on a plane while reading and first noticed the connection with his words when I laughed so loud I embarrassed myself. The next outburst was also unexpected. Tears were flowing down my face. The stewardess didn't seem to notice, yet I didn't want to cry while sitting in the aisle seat of a commercial flight. Once I did, however, I realized how pent up I had been. I needed to cry. Life is hard but love lasts long.

Untamed isn't a book asking for permission or agreement. Are you okay with that? Are you okay with swimming in water so deep you become less sure about your swim stroke and start to lean into the waves? Say yes to the dance. Say yes to the dream. Say yes to love. Say yes to the wonder. I recommend this book for the young and old, the faithful and the faithless, the skeptic and the saved. This isn't about invasion. This is about surrender.

—Scott Crowder
Singer/songwriter and leader of DreamHouse Church
Newport News, VA
JesusLoves757.com

Jason writes of a life lived in the tension of the unseen yet seen. It is a life of faith, and we are all called to it. *Untamed* is an invitation to live in His Kingdom as little children even as we struggle with our adult minds and circumstances. Jason has beautifully expressed the dichotomy of living in both worlds with a trusting heart.

—Pat Bank
House of Healing Ministries
Campbellsville, KY

Jason Clark has gifted us with a book that has life on it! In *Untamed* you will find much more than a fine-sounding theological construct. You will receive revelation on how 21st century Kingdom carriers must live if they are to fulfill their divine mandate to bring the will of our heavenly Father to earth, for the sake of His glory. When the last page of this book is turned, while the weight of its content still rests in your hands, take time to listen—I am sure you will hear the Holy Spirit say, "Now go and change a generation!"

—MARK APPLEYARD
Lead pastor, Crossroads Church
Waxhaw, NC

The adventure of being! In *Untamed* Jason has hit at the heart of what the church needs most—sons and daughters! He nails the simple yet profound truth that we were created to *be* partners with God, not mere servants that are measured by what we *do*. The God of the universe is offering to partner with us to see our dreams come true, and offering us the opportunity to partner with Him to see His Kingdom come! This book is a defibrillator to the dead heart that has ravaged the church. Prepare to be brought back to life as you read!

—JUSTIN AND JESSICA COLLINS
Senior pastors, Vanguard Church
Tonawanda, NY

Untamed reaches into the depths of the human soul, taking an honest and refreshing look at what it means to have a personal relationship with the living God. Jason confronts "religiosity" and brings Christianity back to the lifestyle Jesus set before His disciples of radical love and extreme faith. This book will renew your passion for the type of radical Christianity needed in the world today.

—JAMES KRECHNYAK JR.
Church planter and author, *Through the Wildernes*
and *Living the Dream*
Ireland

Beautiful and thought provoking, but more than that. *Untamed* will unleash in you the desire to boldly go where you were destined to go and achieve the dreams God planted in your heart even against seemingly impossible odds. It will give you the awareness that Jesus is with you every step along the journey of life.

—Julia Loren
Author, *When God Says Yes: His Promise & Provision
When You Need It Most*

I read it, loved it, laughed with it, and cried in it. My prayer is that God would find on earth not a generation of the selfish and comfortable, the independent and domesticated, but a generation of the totally surrendered and untamed. May I be one of them.

—Mika Yrjola
Senior pastor, Saalem Christian Church
Helsinki, Finland

Forty years ago, *The Edge of Adventure* by Keith Miller and Bruce Larson stood on top of the Christian best-seller list. The authors said one of the chief marks of emotional and spiritual health is a willingness to take risk. Well, a generation later comes *Untamed*. Jason Clark is living the adventure, taking bold risks, pushing every envelope, all in search of the story—the story of God's inbreaking, Christ's transforming, the Spirit's empowering work in their lives and in the lives of those around them. Consider yourself warned, your life will become less boring just for reading this!

—Jack Haberer
Senior Pastor, Vanderbilt Presbyterian Church
Author, *God Views* and *Living the Presence of the Spirit*
Naples, FL

Jason Clark is a man sent from God. He has been wired to help us see aspects of God that we need to see, but that we may not have seen on our own. Like the apostle John, he urgently declares what he has both seen and heard. *Untamed* is his declaration, and reading it is an adventure. Hang on—this will stretch you.

—DICK GROUT
Director of music, Elim Bible Institute
Lima, NY

"The Kingdom is at hand, it is near." Jason shows us how to grab hold of this truth in a way that transforms us, that we might transform the world. *Untamed* brings us to the conclusion that taking risks with Father God is the only safe thing to do. This book gives purpose to the scary process of walking by faith.

—JEFFREY WATSON
Lead pastor, Newsong Church
Cornelius, NC

UNTAMED

DESTINY IMAGE BOOKS BY JASON CLARK

Prone to Love

UNTAMED

A FOOL'S GUIDE TO
SURRENDERED FAITH

JASON CLARK

© Copyright 2015–Jason Clark

All rights reserved. This book is protected by the copyright laws of the United States of America. This book may not be copied or reprinted for commercial gain or profit. The use of short quotations or occasional page copying for personal or group study is permitted and encouraged. Permission will be granted upon request. Unless otherwise identified, Scripture quotations are taken from the HOLY BIBLE, NEW INTERNATIONAL VERSION®, Copyright © 1973, 1978, 1984 International Bible Society. Used by permission of Zondervan. All rights reserved. Scripture quotations marked NKJV are taken from the New King James Version. Copyright © 1982 by Thomas Nelson, Inc. Used by permission. All rights reserved. Scripture quotations marked KJV are taken from the King James Version. Scripture quotations marked NASB are taken from the NEW AMERICAN STANDARD BIBLE®, Copyright © 1960, 1962, 1963, 1968, 1971, 1972, 1973, 1975, 1977, 1995 by The Lockman Foundation. Used by permission. Scripture quotations marked MSG are taken from *The Message*. Copyright © 1993, 1994, 1995, 1996, 2000, 2001, 2002. Used by permission of NavPress Publishing Group. Scripture quotations marked NLT are taken from the Holy Bible, New Living Translation, copyright 1996, 2004. Used by permission of Tyndale House Publishers, Wheaton, Illinois 60189. All rights reserved. All emphasis within Scripture quotations is the author's own.
DESTINY IMAGE® PUBLISHERS, INC.

P.O. Box 310, Shippensburg, PA 17257-0310

"Promoting Inspired Lives."

Previously published as *Surrendered and Untamed* by Baker Publishing
Previous ISBN: 978-0-8010-1376-8

This book and all other Destiny Image and Destiny Image Fiction books are available at Christian bookstores and distributors worldwide.

Cover design by Christian Rafetto

For more information on foreign distributors, call 717-532-3040.

Reach us on the Internet: www.destinyimage.com.

ISBN 13 TP: 978-0-7684-0763-1

ISBN 13 eBook: 978-0-7684-0764-8

For Worldwide Distribution, Printed in the U.S.A.

1 2 3 4 5 6 7 8 / 19 18 17 16 15

Dedication

To my dad and mom who have lived an untamed faith in such a way to empower this boy to live the same.

Acknowledgements

Thank you Father, Your love is so good! That I would know more…

Karen, my best friend. Maddy, Ethan and Eva, you're my favorites! My parents who've always modeled believing, I can't help but love God more because of how you both live—thank you! Aimee and Eric, Joel and Megan, Josiah and Ben. JV, Cindy, Kathleen, Aaron, Bobby and Martin. You guys are the best family ever, I love our story!

Joel, for dreaming with me and never doubting.

Eric Perry, the great friend; Jeremy Cole, the great encourager. Shawn Ring, the great visionary; Joel Carver, the great adventurer. Scott Crowder, the great catalyst! The Perrys, Rings, Carvers, Coles, Crowders, and Harnishes—men and families with Kingdom influence. All the friends who have been life to my family and me over the years. We love you guys!

Gary Winston, thanks so much for your brilliant cover design. We love the Winstons!

Lee Hough who took a chance and believed in us and everyone at Alive Communications, as well as Chad Allen and everyone at Baker Books for your part in the first edition entitled *Surrendered & Untamed*.

John Blasé for the gift of refinement. Mykela Krieg, Ronda Ranalli, Ryan Adair and everyone at Destiny Image.

Those "Fathers in the Faith" who have influenced me—my Dad, Bill Johnson, Dan Mohler, Kris Vallotton, Graham Cooke, Danny Silk, Erwin McManus, Dick Grout.

Scott Crowder, Coldplay, Mumford & Sons, John Mark McMillan, Envy Corps, Anthony Skinner, The Killers, U2, Arcade Fire, Sigur Ros, Brian and Jenn Johnson, Imogen Heap, Mutemath, Band of a Thousand, The Fire Theft, Jonathan and Melissa Helser, Ben Howard, Bon Iver, Josh Baldwin, The Veils, The National, Jacob Early, M83, Hey Rosetta and many more for the sounds of momentum.

And coffee. Thank you baristas, be blessed.

Contents

A Warning and an Invitation

I know this may look like an ordinary book...but it really should come with a warning label in bold letters that says: **Untamed will disrupt your world in the best of ways.**

My friend Jason Clark is your warrior-poet storyteller for this not safe, yet good journey. Though I've not yet met him, I feel a deep bond. Primarily because his life and words have drawn me exponentially closer to God's heart. Okay, that and the fact that we share a love of strong coffee, spicy food and 80s television shows.

My copy of *Untamed* is dog-eared, tear stained, and almost completely highlighted in neon orange. The first time I finished the book, I felt I'd been simultaneously struck by lightning, embraced in a lover's touch, and feasted at God's banquet table. The stories stretched my faith, quickened my pulse, and increased my hunger to live a far more untamed and reckless life for God.

Perhaps most, Jason helped me grow in my understanding of what it means to live as a son of God. The thought that my Father has rescued me not just for service and productivity but for presence and intimacy...well, that changes everything. As Jason says,

"It's personal friendship with our Creator that satisfies our souls and makes us whole."

This book is also an intimate invitation that should come signed with these handwritten words:

Untamed will disrupt your world in the best of ways.

God first led me to this book when I wasn't looking for it. He somehow did the same for you. I think it's because God knows once we experience untamed intimacy with Him, we'll never be satisfied with small dreams, safe faith, and simple prayers. That is the invitation.

The world may call this approach to living reckless and foolish. But really now, is there any better kind of fool to be?

—ALLEN ARNOLD
Ransomed Heart Ministries

Introduction

My dad has stories, lots of childhood rememberings. Many of them include his brothers. Most of those include fist throwing, rock throwing, and even knife throwing—all in good fun, at least, at the beginning. And many of these childhood stories have some small amounts of bloodshed.

And then there is the pretty story about an RV trailer.

One summer the brothers Clark had a vision. And it was beautiful. It was the best things brothers dream together. It was about the wide-open places, it was filled with the promise of adventure, pioneering and discovery. The brothers would build an RV trailer. This trailer would be spectacular, it would be pulled behind their dad's 1961 Hillman and in this RV trailer they would see the world!

The Clark boys gathered together to make the vision a reality and for several days there was brotherly love and goodwill toward all. They practically lived in the back shed behind the house. First they built the trailer bed out of a few boards. Then they constructed the wheels—also out of wood. There'd need to be a bed, and a chair. And of course windows and maybe a table for breakfast. There would need to be a stove to cook the eggs.

Wood, they had in abundance; the sky was the limit.

While they built, they envisioned the open road and the trailer grew in their hearts and minds as well as in the shed. They were believers living in the passionate hope of a future filled with wonder. It was a beautiful time, each day a new idea added life to the journey. And as the brothers worked they forgot their fists, rocks, and knives. Sure there were disagreements, but the promise of wide-open places was too grand to allow petty infighting to stall the completion.

At first they were just going to travel down the road a ways. Maybe camp at the Provincial park outside of London, Ontario. But as the trailer amassed in size, so too did their plans. Soon they were traveling to distant exotic places like Niagara Falls and even further, the Rockies, the Grand Canyon, Mt. Everest. The promise of adventure and fulfillment and joy and life added strength to their hands and they worked through lunches and well past dusk.

Finally the day arrived. It was finished. It was beautiful!

Their dad's car was parked in the driveway. It was time to unveil the RV trailer and begin the true adventure.

And here is where conflict enters the narrative; here is where the story takes an unexpected, disappointing and yet oddly familiar turn. This is the part of the story we have all experienced in one way or another.

Not one of the brothers had given any thought to the size of the shed doors in comparison to the size of the RV trailer.

The trailer was too big! Or maybe it was actually the other way around, maybe the shed doors were too small. Or maybe a Rambler was never going to be able to pull an RV trailer, or maybe wood wheels were never going to work. Maybe the vision was too grand and the dream too foolish. Maybe the promise of wide-open places were never meant to be realized.

The story of the RV trailer ended poorly. The experience that had begun with sincere wonder, and faithful expectation, and hard work, ended in tragic disappointment.

And yet, you know as well as I, the promise of the open road never stopped calling. It never does.

We are born to discover a life, full and whole, and true. We all have open-road promises from God—His Kingdom in and through us. We have been designed for the grand adventure, invited to live and move and have our being in a landscape that is every bit as measureless as its Creator. We have been designed to know Love and personify it. Our hearts are designed to know joy and love and laughter. Our minds are formed to envision and dream of impossibilities becoming possible. Our eyes created to be filled with the wonder of vast landscapes, and the glory of a loved one's smile.

The life of a believer is a wide-open love affair, an untamed adventure, His Kingdom established in our lives. In God, we are promised Niagara Falls, the Rockies, the Grand Canyon, Mt. Everest. The wide-open places—it's our birthright.

And yet, we all will experience shed doors that are just too small, seasons where the open road is more theory than reality. We all will have vision destroyed by life-crushing disappointment. We all will experience the soul-ravaging conflict in our narrative. And when this happens we are presented with a choice.

Believe or don't.

We have been invited into a life of foolish surrendered faith; a life where we design and build trailers out of wood in sheds with doors that are way too small. We have been invited on a journey of envisioning, dreaming, and trusting. And we have been invited to continue believing and in so doing discover an always-goods loving God and His measureless one-of-a-kind promise—a life sure in His affection.

And I am learning that this kind of believing will rip a hole so large in the side of our shed that we will find ourselves halfway to Niagara Falls before we even know what's happened.

I am absolutely convinced that we have not yet seen, on this earth, the wonders of believers living in the fullness of their promises.

This book is my foolish and untamed story, my discovery of the wide-open places. It is my faith story. It is filled with sheds doors that are too small and RV trailers that are too big, and it is brimming with my discovery of a good God and adventure and fulfillment and joy and life. This book may even be an expression of my wide-open believing. I pray it inspires and empowers you. May we all discover our story in His and may the world be forever changed!

Blessings
—Jason

Chapter 1

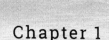 The Promise

The Polar Express

Maybe you got tired of living stale
Playing safe while all your ships set off to sail

I was sitting in a packed theater beside a three-year-old boy named Ethan Wilde. Ethan is my son. We were about to watch *The Polar Express.* I was a little distracted because we had just moved to North Carolina, pretty sure God asked us to make the move—but just *pretty* sure. We had spent our savings and were now digging into our "good credit." We were beyond strapped, and spending $8.00 for the afternoon matinee caused an anxious voice in my head to suggest that I might be crazy.

A thirty-year-old man with a wife and two kids isn't usually 100 percent certain of much, but I was about 97 percent convinced I was to spend all my time and resources birthing a ministry, which I would later discover was a lifestyle. I would learn my true ministry was simply believing my heavenly Father loves me and He is always good. God had invited me to believe, to trust Him, to stay the course.

But as the money flew out of our savings account, I was more than a little worried. In fact, I was terrified.

Dave Ramsey's evaluation would have been...uh, financial suicide. Now I know Dave Ramsey has helped many people out of financial ruin, but this was between me and another Savior—it had nothing to do with financial responsibility. This was about irresponsible, unsound, downright foolish trust. I had been invited by my Father into an opportunity to believe, and it was stretching my faith. But I'll return to this a little later...

Back to *The Polar Express*. If you haven't seen it, then try to—it's wonderful. It's about a young boy who, while growing up, loses his ability to believe in Father God—I mean, Santa Claus. Fortunately, Jesus, the Holy Spirit, and the Father—I mean three variations of Tom Hanks—band together to guide the boy back into believing. I realize that may sound confusing, but stick with me for a moment.

It's Christmas Eve and instead of dreaming of the best day of the year, the boy is in his bedroom agonizing over the universal question: Does God...sorry, I mean Santa Claus, really exist? The boy used to believe, but now in the mind of this blossoming adult, a rotund, bearded jolly man delivering presents to the entire world's population in one night seems impossible. Add in flying reindeer, elves, a North Pole toy factory—it all feels completely foolish. The boy is in danger of becoming an unbelieving grown-up. No, worse than that—a realist.

And then a deep rumbling. It grows louder until it fills his room and even leaps into our theater seats. Like an earthquake, it shakes and rattles his shelf of sports trophies. The boy creeps over to his window, looks out, and what to his wondering eyes should appear? An enormous train decked in his front yard.

Dressed in his pajamas and rubber rain boots, he cautiously walks out to the train and meets Jesus...I'm sorry, I mean a train conductor played by Tom Hanks. The conductor says, "Well...are you coming?" That's a question worth remembering.

The boy is in awe. He really wants to get on the train, but at the same time the idea terrifies him. Finally, as the locomotive begins to inch forward, and as the opportunity begins to slip away, his young heart wins out and he takes the outstretched hand of the conductor.

And so the journey begins. Absolutely anything can happen, and it does—a grand adventure filled with mountaintops and frozen lakes and howling wolves and dancing waiters balancing hot chocolate. It's exciting and dangerous all at the same time. Along the way the boy meets a ghost who again oddly resembles Tom Hanks, or was it the Holy Ghost?

After several breathtaking adventures, the train reaches its final destination—the North Pole. There are elves everywhere, and music, dancing, and singing. It is truly a magical place. I plan to go there some day.

Everyone is awaiting Santa's arrival, which signals the official start of Christmas. Most of the elves are singing Christmas songs with rowdy enthusiasm. Some are whispering, "Is he here?" and others are shouting, "Can you see him?" The anticipation is almost unbearable.

The reindeer harnessed to Santa's sleigh are playfully wild. Their master is coming. They can sense it. The sleigh bells on the reindeer are ringing and all who believe in Santa can hear them, their pristine crystal tones adding to the beautiful, chaotic expectation that has filled the atmosphere. All the children who made the journey are there too and no less enthused. The air is electric with the anticipation of something so good.

And then there is the boy, his unbelief and anxiety still very evident and at tension with his surroundings. He had all but decided Santa was not real and yet he wants—with his whole heart—to be wrong. He wants to believe. Surrounded by a sea of believers, the boy dares to hope; in fact, hope is everywhere, and it's contagious. Hope is like that—it expects more, it promises good things to come, it encourages surrendered participation. If you let it, hope will lead you into some wild, transforming, and world-changing adventures.

A slow hush falls on the crowd, and all eyes became focused on a building at the end of the square. The giant doors burst open. There is a bright light and within the doorframe, a silhouette. Suddenly the whole square erupts. "There he is!" shouts an elf. "I see him!" says one of the girls. But the boy, pressed by the crowd, can't see Santa and still can't hear the sleigh bells.

Desperate, the boy jumps and presses his way through the sea of elves to the front. And then, there he is, gloriously shining, Father God…I'm sorry, I mean Santa Claus, who is also played by, you guessed it, Tom Hanks.

Suddenly the boy hears everything: the sleigh bells, the worshiping elves, the celebrating kids, the dancing reindeer. And I'm sitting beside my son, and I'm desperately trying to hide my face from the little girl on the other side of me. Why? Because I'm bawling my eyes out and whispering, "I believe, I believe, I believe…I love You, Father, and I believe."

You see, I've been given a promise from God, a promise to know Him and be known by Him, a promise of hopes realized, a promise to be transformed, a promise of dreaming with Him, a promise to create, to live a *greater works* life, to change the world. But as you know, life moves at a steady pace, and sometimes bad things happen: disappointments and tragedy, failure and waiting. And along the way it seems holding onto His promises has proved to be rather difficult. This world is a busy and noisy place, and it's easy to wake up one day and find I'm just not sure anymore, believing has become a lost art, deferred hope has made me heartsick, faith seems impossible, even foolish, and the promises of God have become a mountain that seems unscalable. In fact, His promises have often felt like a cruel dream—the harder I try to summit, the farther the peak is from me.

But, like the boy, I have been learning *how* to believe, *how* to keep His promises alive in my heart. And I am discovering the only way to live the "God-promised life" is to take the foolish untamed journey with the Promise Giver. I have said yes to His invitation.

In the movie it took the conductor, the ghost, and Santa all working together to woo the child to believe once again. One man played all three characters, a trinity working in unison, until ultimately the boy made the decision to believe. The boy's heart had wanted to believe from the very start. And that desire was enough to draw him into the perilous, thrilling, and faith-inspiring journey.

Consider the possibility that Jesus is asking you the very same question: "Well…are you coming?"

The Gas Attendant

Up and away, up in a hope-filled night
You climbed away, awake for the first time

I got my first job at a co-op. A mini Wal-Mart of sorts, it even had a gas station in the parking lot. Lucky for me. My dad had driven me there to apply and had assured Bill, the manager, I could be trusted. I explained to Bill how I could easily ride my ten-speed to work, how it made "perfect sense," and so at the age of fifteen for $5.50 an hour (Canadian), I became a gas attendant.

I remember this job well: cold nights where I was forced to either stand outside in the brisk fresh air or sit in the 5 x 10 ft heated cubicle with my two easygoing pot-smoking coworkers. But Bill the manager was anything but easygoing. This was probably due to the fact he was a middle-aged man managing pot-smoking teenagers who were pumping gas. He was almost always mad at someone or something; he coped by yelling at us. So when the sweet old lady came in to fill up her brand-new Cadillac and asked me to top off her oil, I didn't want to bother Bill with absurd questions such as, "Where does the oil go?" I did what any fifteen-year-old boy would boldly do. I guessed wrong.

About a half hour later the sweet old lady was back and she seemed to be having steering problems. "I just don't understand it," she said. "The steering wheel is very hard to turn and it only started happening shortly after I left you." I boldly said what any fifteen-year-old boy would say: "It must be bad gas."

One would think my gas attendant career was over before it had even been given a fighting chance. But four years later, I was again being driven by my dad to apply for a job as a gas attendant. This time I lived just south of Rochester, New York. I was a freshman attending Elim Bible Institute.

Elim is a Bible college, not a seminary. I feel I must make this absolutely clear because several seminary graduates have felt duty bound to inform me of the differences between the two. So we're clear, right? A Bible college does not a seminary make.

I went to Bible college because that's where I thought I'd find "it"—my promise. You see, at the age of five, kneeling at the coffee table one sunny Tuesday afternoon with my mom, I asked Jesus to come into my heart. And Jesus did. Then God did something that still astounds me: He made me a promise.

My heavenly Father—the One who made heaven and earth, who created the infinite stars and can count the sand on the ocean floor—made *me* a promise. It was the first of many to come, but it was also the most profound. On that Tuesday long ago, God promised that He has and will always love me. He promised His love was always good, He would always be with me, and His presence would always be in me—my heart would become His home forever.

And you know what? I believed Him. And it was a grand believing; the kind children are famous for. My understanding was simple and my trust was limitless. God is love and it was more than enough. I had faith, I knew my life was special, and that I was designed to live in Him and through Him and for Him. I inherently believed He would lead me to great things, a life of adventure that was marked by the miraculous.

I have since heard the promise referred to as *destiny* or *purpose*. Those words are good, but I still love the word *promise*. I think it best tells the story. Promise suggests there is more to a life of faith than hard work and chance. It hints at relationship.

Now back to pumping gas as a job for the second time.

In January, in upstate New York, it's dark by 5:00 p.m. and below freezing by 5:30. On this—my first night at the job—it was about five degrees with a wind chill somewhere in the minus ten department. My new coworker and I were warming up inside our little 5 × 10 foot heated cubicle (no pot this time) as a black Volvo pulled up to the pump. I had filled up the last ten cars and was positive it wasn't my turn, but my coworker said, "You go ahead and get this one. That way we can be sure you know what you're doing."

I looked at him just long enough to let him know I thought he was an idiot—and then headed out into the frozen night, my lungs immediately icing over. The lady in the car rolled her window down an inch and said, "Fill it up, please," and then quickly rolled it back up with a look of sympathy.

As I stomped my feet to keep them warm and wiped my nose with the back of my hand, I thought, "This sucks! But God wants me here, it's all a part of His beautiful promise for me." Okay, I'm not certain I thought the second part. In fact, I didn't think the second part as I was freezing my tail off.

But I did think of it later in my warm bed while talking with my heavenly Father. I knew He had a plan for me and this Bible college was where I would discover the grand adventure, where I would find the promised life of significance that was filled with love and beauty and probably a little fame too.

The discovery of my promise became my pursuit. It's what kept me pumping gas in western New York on desperately cold nights in order to earn enough money to afford a Bible college education that later couldn't be compared to a seminary education. All this gas pumping was just an obstacle I had to overcome, a hurdle toward significance, a means to my end, my promise, the "it."

The days turned to months and the months to years, and the years threatened decades. Pumping gas became waiting tables, playing in a band, leading small groups at church, working in masonry, leading worship on Sunday mornings, painting houses, working with a missions organizations, working in construction, and....

In each season it felt as if I were waiting for my story to begin, for my promise to become a reality, but it never seemed any closer. Along the way I gained clarity on who I was, I discovered giftings and grace, and I received glimpses of my promise. But time and distance, along with disappointment, misunderstanding, disaster, and, sadly, other fatigued Christians, undermined my trust in the goodness of God's love. My faith subtly eroded, and with it, my hope. Believing became hard and then painful.

My promise, that once larger-than-life anticipation, slowly became a burden until it haunted me like a heartsick ghost. Where once I discovered my promise in a song, a book, a movie, or a sermon, now it used those things to taunt me. My heart grew heavy with disappointment and my promise mocked me with hope deferred. I grew weary. "How many more cars do I have to fill up, Lord? How many more Bible classes do I have to take? How many more houses must I paint? How many more obstacles? How much longer must I chase 'it'?"

I lost my faith. Please get this: I didn't stop being a Christian, I just stopped believing; to me, it was an exercise in foolishness. Then, several years ago, I had my own *Polar Express* moment. It happened late one night, only days before I watched the movie with my son. Karen and the kids were in bed when God spoke to my heart. He asked me a simple and yet terrifying question: "Do you trust Me?"

I sensed His question carried with it an invitation into grand adventure, but also into great risk. I had a sense there was a mind-renewing journey ahead if I would answer yes. His question was the extended hand, an invitation to take a journey into believing again. Like the boy in *The Polar Express*, I was terrified, and like the boy, my young heart won out. I took His hand. Sitting on my living room floor, out loud I said, "Yes, I trust You." I felt Jesus immediately respond to my heart, "Then believe."

I determined from that night forward that there would only be a yes in my heart. It was the beginning of a new grand adventure. And on the journey, my perspective about God and life has undergone a radical shift. Up to that point, I had spent my life chasing my promise, the elusive "it." Every experience, including the jobs I described, were a pursuit of "it." But since that conversation with Father, Son, and Holy Spirit, I have begun to live in the revelation that I was not born into His Kingdom, adopted into His family, and my heart made His home so I could discover my promise. Rather, it was so I could surrender my promise and discover the Promise Giver. It's not "I" but "Him."

I am no longer chasing an ever-elusive promise but embracing Him. I'm no longer waiting for my story to begin; I'm smack in the middle of it.

In the beginning, God dreamed and a world was born. A love story began. Since the beginning of this story, the all-powerful Creator of the heavens and the earth has pursued us, loved us, died for us, risen for us, and invited us to live within the context of His love. From day one, our Father has purposed sons and daughters to discover and then live sure in His love. That's our story, our promise.

We are invited to discover who He is, that He is good, trustworthy, kind and so much more—it's called faith.

There has always been one question He has asked of us, echoed down the corridors of history: "Do you trust Me?" Or as Tom Hanks put it, "Well…are you coming?"

The Promise

I turn my face, to a blazing son
Your glory falls, Your Kingdom comes

Peter is one of my favorite fellas from the Bible. I can often find my story in his. He was a favorite of Jesus as well. Peter often gets a bad rap for his impulsive, headstrong, and occasional disastrous conclusions, but I love him for his ardent and fierce trust. I love him because he wasn't afraid to risk, to try even if he got it wrong.

I imagine him as that confident kid in high school you wanted to hang out with, at least until the cops came. He was the cool kid who drove the muscle car way too fast; it was awesome until he crashed it into a tree stump while doing donuts in the Johnson's field. He was the fearless kid who jumped off the sixty-foot cliff edge into the reservoir while all the girls watched. It was exhilarating until he hit the rocks on the way down, broke his leg, and spent the rest of the summer on crutches.

Peter was a pioneer, a revolutionary, and wasn't afraid to go first. He let everyone else know it could be done, albeit, better and with more style. Peter encouraged and empowered following generations into believing.

There is this one story where Peter shows us the way into our future through his own radical discovery of his. He found his promise in the discovery of the Promise Giver, and in so doing showed us the keys to discover ours.

Jesus, walking one day with His disciples, asked a question, "Who do you say I am?" And Peter rushed in, "You're the Christ, the Messiah, the Son of the living God." Jesus responded to Peter, *"You didn't get that answer out of books or from teachers. My Father in heaven, God Himself, let you in on this secret of who I really am"* (Matt. 16:17 MSG).

Now here's the deal: everywhere Jesus went, every breath He ever took, every smile and tear, everything He did, every word He spoke, was meant to do one thing—reveal God as Father. Jesus told the disciples continually that He came to show us the Father. He said, *"If you really knew Me, you would know My Father as well"* (John 14:7), and *"I am in the Father and the Father is in Me"* (John 14:11). So I imagine Jesus was thrilled with Peter's statement as it was directly from Father God. Peter looked at Jesus and met the Father. He got it!

After Jesus let Peter know where his revelation came from, He continued with a personal enlightening message from the Father: *"And now I'm going to tell you who you are, really are. You are Peter, a rock. This is the rock on which I will put together My church, a church so expansive with energy that not even the gates of hell will be able to keep it out"* (Matt. 16:18 MSG).

Can you imagine this scene? Peter, while describing Jesus, meets Father God and is then given his promise. Peter discovered his promise through the discovery of the Promise Giver. But Jesus wasn't finished:

> *And that's not all. You will have complete and free access to God's kingdom, keys to open any and every door: no more barriers between heaven and earth, earth and heaven. A yes on earth is yes in heaven. A no on earth is no in heaven* (Matthew 16:19 MSG).

These verses absolutely astound me. Not only is Peter given his promise in the form of his identity, but he is then given his promise in the form of his inheritance as a son of God. It was as if Jesus were saying, "Peter, as you keep your eyes on Me, you will discover there are no barriers, no measureable limits to My promises—all impossibilities become possibilities. When you keep your eyes on Me, you won't live chasing an ever elusive promise, you will live smack in the middle it. When you see Me, you can see your true self, and all the promises I have given you. And these promises will powerfully transform you, the lives around you, and the lives to come."

This story tells us that if we want to know who we are, if we want to know what we are called to do, if we want to know what we have access to, if we want to know and live smack in the middle of our promise, then we must keep our eyes on the Promise Giver. One revelation of Father, Son, and Holy Spirit brings more clarity regarding call, promise, identity, destiny, power, and authority than a lifetime of anything else, including Bible study and good messages—*"You didn't get this from a book or teachers...."*

I'm not suggesting Bible study and good messages aren't valuable, I'm simply noting they should always lead to Jesus and reveal the Father. It's an encounter with God that reveals our promise and releases the keys to personal and then worldwide transformation.

Peter had many more bumbling adventures after he received his promise from the Father. One time he put engine oil in the steering column of a kind old lady's car...no, wait...Peter continued to display what getting it wrong looked like. However, he also continued to believe and trust, and he kept his eyes on Jesus and a yes in his heart. Along the way his vision of Jesus became clearer and he continued to be transformed.

Many years after Jesus had risen and ascended, *"people brought the sick into the streets and laid them on beds and mats so that at least Peter's shadow might fall on some of them as he passed by"* (Acts 5:15). Peter's shadow had authority to heal. The same Peter who got it wrong so many times before discovered a believing that led to a personal transformation that ended up changing the world.

I haven't always fully known what my promise looks like, I haven't always been able to describe it, but I am learning, and I think it's a little like *"God's kingdom, keys to open any and every door: no more barriers between heaven and earth, earth and heaven. A yes on earth is yes in heaven. A no on earth is no in heaven"* (Matt. 16:19 MSG). I am discovering that if I'm willing to surrender—my heart for His—I get to engage and experience all His heart offers. I think that's what untamed living is all about—coalescing my promise with His purpose, His love.

I believe we all have a one-of-a-kind promise from God: His Kingdom of heaven birthed within us. This promise is unique to every individual, is discovered in a revelation of Father, Son, and Holy Spirit, and lives in our hearts. And His promises are greater than anything we could ask for or even imagine. His promises are invitations to believe, step out, risk, trust, and fail; to discover Jesus, be transformed, and walk in the authority of heaven.

"Who do you say that I am?" Jesus is still asking us this question today. It's an extended hand to take an untamed adventure, to live a world-changing faith. And it sounds different for all of us. For me it came in the question, "Do you trust Me?" or "Well...are you coming?"

The Eternal Optimist

I've felt a sense of urgency
A lion come alive in me, in revelation of Your love

Hi, my name is Jason and I'm a recovering realist.

I chased my promise for so long that I lost sight of the Promise Giver. I became exhausted, unmotivated, and unsure. I lost hope and life became random and dull. In one sense, I still did what I thought

God had created me to do, but it no longer held joy. I started filtering every experience through an attitude of hopelessness, until every bump in the road was expected, while every triumph was fleeting. Somewhere along the way I stopped believing.

I became a realist because that's what happens when you stop believing. Realism is the only option for a saved unbeliever. That's right, I became a faithless Christian. I began living a life where the glass was neither half full nor half empty. It was just half.

I'm afraid realism is living in the kingdom of man. While realism can often appear to be practical, respectable, and even wise, it's simply unbelief. Realism is just a socially accepted form of pessimism, a kind of kryptonite for those who want to engage their promise.

Realism says, "If you don't have the money, God must not be in it… If you're sick, it must be God's will—maybe He is trying to teach you something… If it's dangerous, it probably shouldn't be attempted… If you're poor, then get a job… If you want to minister, go to Bible college or seminary… If you're offending someone's sensibilities, then stop." It basically says that whatever you do, be careful or you may come out looking like an idiot; or worse, you may experience disappointment, and you may even fail. In short, if at all possible, avoid risk.

Realism will always promote the idea of building monuments but never empower movement. Realism will say, "We must protect what God gave us; we need to be responsible and careful regarding our 'Christian walk.' We need to be respectable, nice, and safe." And, oh yeah, did I mention frustrated, fed up, and bored out of our minds? Or how about aimless, empty, and miserable? And don't forget powerless, faithless, and tamed.

Believing is about living from another Kingdom—that of heaven. Believing inspires action, births revelation, and yields miracles. A realist would see a blind man and say he can't see, end of story. But when Jesus walked the earth, the blind saw, the lame walked, the deaf heard, Lazarus died twice, and Jesus told death, "Thanks, but no!" From what I can tell, God is not a realist. He is the Eternal Optimist who has called all of us to live eternally optimistically with Him. He has invited us into a believing lifestyle.

Believing is keeping our eyes on the prize; it's forward living, faith in motion. Belief is good, but for it to grow it needs to be nurtured by a believing lifestyle. *"I tell you the truth, anyone who believes in Me will do the same works I have done, and even greater works, because I am going to be with the Father"* (John 14:12 NLT). Jesus's whole message on earth points to a "greater works than these" lifestyle. Greater works is His promise to us.

The promise—your promise and mine—is one of a Spirit-led life, a Spirit-breathed life, a life of seeing where the Father moves and moving with Him. What does this greater works promise look like? Well, I can't see all of it, but I'm learning that it lives in my heart and can be discovered in my dreams—particularly the dreams that most excite and most terrify me. I am also learning the only way to see more of it, to engage it, is to say yes to the journey and develop a believing heart. It's the journey where I am given opportunity to trust and then discover the Promise Giver.

This journey is a counterculture revolution. It has often appeared crazy, financially irresponsible, unsound, and downright foolish. At times it has blemished my reputation. It has carried with it a stigma, and I have tasted the sting of reproach from the church, friends, and even family.

We live in a culture that has deified the mind. Yes, God gave us the intellect, but let me make this clear: the mind must yield to the believing heart. God never sees a glass as half empty, or even as half full; it could have one drop and He would see it as overflowing. I am discovering that there is a way to live from His perspective.

Jesus told us to love the Lord our God with all our heart, soul, strength, and mind (see Luke 10:27)—there is a reason it's in that order. They all work together, but the heart must come first. Jesus lives in our hearts, not in our minds. Believing is risky, it really does cost everything, and it often doesn't add up in the mind as something we can see. But faith, after all, is the essence of things unseen (see Heb. 11:1).

I'm afraid I would still be a realist today if not for the wild yearning in my heart for more, and for the willingness to say yes to His invitation to trust. God in His grace and faithfulness has intervened in some very godlike ways. He's used pot-smoking coworkers, freezing cold temperatures, Bible college and endless vocations to bring me along.

Then there are those wild believers who have affected my life—men and women who modeled godly optimism by living lives marked by the dangerous favor of God. Some of them have been flesh and blood, like my dad and mom, my wife, Karen, and my kids Madeleine, Ethan, and Eva, while others have been enfleshed in stories, like God-the-conductor-Tom-Hanks on a silver screen asking "the" question:

"Well…are you coming?"

Chapter 2

He Loves Me Best

God is always speaking to me, and to you as well. I've discovered His voice in nature, by way of friends, family, and elders. I have discovered Him through some of my favorite authors. I've also found Him in a song or movie. But mostly I know Him through that gentle whisper in my heart (see 1 Kings 19:12). His voice confirms what I've read in my Bible, that He loves me and His love is always good—*always*.

This may be a revolutionary concept—that a loving Father, the Creator of the universe, is speaking to each and every one of us, every day, all of the time. What makes it even more amazing is regardless of how the message is delivered, our heavenly Father is always saying one thing: "I love you." And that is always followed by one question: "Do you believe Me?"

Sinbad, Seacrest, and Paper Cuts

There is a love beyond understanding
There is a grace that consumes

I was already tired and we were only seven hours into a thirty-three-hour trip. My dad and I were on our way to China to look into some business opportunities. We left Charlotte, North Carolina, in the afternoon. "Why start a thirty-three-hour trip in the afternoon?" you may ask. I don't know, and neither did the lady at the airline counter.

We were standing in LAX, and though I was tired, I was excited as well. Last time I went through LAX, I got to meet Sinbad. Well, I didn't actually meet him; more like saw him, which is practically the same thing. He was in line to check his luggage.

He really is a funny guy. He didn't do anything funny while I was watching him, which was a little disappointing, but I imagine it's hard to be funny all the time. Plus, it *was* early and everyone knows comedians aren't funny in the morning. I bet he's hilarious after lunch.

It gets better, because after I saw Sinbad, I saw Ryan Seacrest, who hosts *American Idol*, as well as virtually every other show on TV. I actually did meet him; we sat in first class together. I know what you're thinking. "Why is Jason sitting in first class? Is he *that guy*? You know, the fella in first class who looks down his nose at all the second-class rabble, the saps headed to coach."

Maybe I am. Maybe I like entering the plane first. Maybe I enjoy sitting Indian style in a comfortable leather seat while the common folk are trotted through first class. Maybe I like having a curtain separate me from the cacophony of noises and smells wafting off the masses in second class. And maybe I enjoy a nice Chardonnay while speaking in high English with the cream of world citizenry. But probably it was because the flight was overbooked and I got bumped.

For that one glorious day I was cultured and civilized and just an all-around better person. I sat in first class and Ryan and I discussed the last show of the season and the new *American Idol*. He was very polite, a nice fella. And I think I held my own; that is to say, I don't think he discerned I had never been there before—in first class.

But I digress. Back to my China trip. I was excited about this journey, not just for the possibility of first class conversations with American icons, but also because I love to travel and we were going to places I had never been before.

The airport in Los Angeles was jam-packed. We were standing in the customs line for international flights, waiting to check our bags. There were about 200 people in front of us, plus the thousands of others who filled our little universe known as Terminal Two. Surrounded by the huddled masses, I began to have one of those feelings I think everyone experiences from time to time. I felt small. With thousands of people moving through that section of the airport every five minutes and the knowledge that we were about to go to a country with a population of over a billion, I suddenly felt insignificant.

I wonder if Sinbad ever feels insignificant? Probably not. But that's just a guess.

While I was standing there feeling "small," I noticed the girl in front of me. She was standing with her back to me, her arms crossed. I could just see the tips of the fingers on her left hand. I noticed her index finger had a tiny paper cut. It was a little inflamed and looked like it could be irritated, but it was nothing serious. Suddenly I felt the presence of my heavenly Father, as if He were standing right next to me. Then He said to my heart, "I was there when that happened. I felt it."

Now, as I mentioned earlier, God is always speaking and sometimes He says the strangest things. This seemed to be one of those times. So I responded to God in my heart. "Father, I can't possibly understand this, my mind can't begin to grasp it. I am just a speck in the universe, a blink of the eye in light of eternity." As I looked around at the thousands of people, I became overwhelmed. Then I prayed. "Father, how many paper cuts are in this place? How many people are here with bigger problems than paper cuts? What would possess You to even point out a small, seemingly insignificant paper cut? How is it possible for me to understand this?"

Then my heavenly Father said, "It's not about your understanding, it's about your believing—believing the absolute goodness that is My love. Do you believe Me?" At that moment I got a glimpse of my Father's heart of love, and I was undone. I could barely compose myself. I was awed by the revelation that His love for the world included paper cuts. To be fair, I'm not sure I truly believed Him. But to be honest, I absolutely wanted to. "Yes, Father, I choose to believe. Now please show me how."

Revelation

Let me find my joy complete
Let me see, oh love, be my sweet witness

Let me tell you how it is between my wife and me. We could be driving down the road or sitting on the couch watching the BBC version of *Sherlock* when suddenly I'm gripped with a revelation of how amazing Karen is. I will remember how she was so patient with our kids earlier in the day, or how she just made me coffee and I didn't even ask for it, and it was the perfect mix of coffee, cream, and sugar. Or how stunning the back of her neck is. I will turn to her and say that simple universal phrase—"I love you"—to which she always responds, "I love you too, gorgeous."

But sometimes in these unveiled moments I'll stop what I'm doing and say, "Karen, I'm feeling it right now—heart, soul, mind, and strength. All of me is loving all of you, right now."

"Right this instant?" she asks, her eyes bright.

"Yes, this exact moment."

"Wow." She smiles. "Now I'm feeling it too!" Often this interaction is followed by an encounter. That is to say, there might be a shared smile or a hug, a kiss, or...well, that's none of your business.

I believe revelation, in the context of a love relationship, always leads to a greater love encounter, a greater intimacy. It is about both being loved and loving. In fact, that's the whole point of revelation. Karen and I have been married twenty years and she is more fascinating to me today than yesterday. The more I know her, the more I want to know her. That's the wonder of revelation—it's a discovery of measureless love.

Karen and I know we love each other, we say it all the time, and we decide to all the time. But these moments of revelation are priceless. They are birthed of a pure surrender, one to another, where everything in the universe aligns and our heart, soul, mind, and strength experience the encounter. In these moments, nothing else matters. In these moments, the truth of our love is purely revealed and is always deepened.

I am convinced when it comes to our relationship with God that revelation is meant to lead to a greater encounter. Revelation means "to remove the veil"; it's the discovery of what's always been there; it's about knowing in greater measure the love of God. I am also convinced there is always more to be revealed and experienced.

I have discovered God's love is the point. It's the very foundation of this world. It's not a vague concept; it's an encounter. We live to know Love...and to become love. We were created to be loved and to love. We are designed for revelation.

He Loves Me Best

Sweet love, come darling, the air is alive,
The time is ripe for you and me

Do you know who wrote the Gospel of John? John did—I looked it up. Do you know that three times in the Gospel of John he refers to himself in the third person? Each time this is revealed as "the *one* Jesus loves" (see John 13:23; 19:26; 21:7). It's almost as if John is saying "Jesus loves me best."

Think about this. If anyone knew God's love, it would be the disciples. John, being one of the twelve, lived with Jesus for three years. They did life together; they laughed, cried, ate, walked, and prayed together. John was there for the miracles, when Jesus healed, delivered, forgave, restored, and made more food out of less. John was there when Jesus was moved with compassion and poured Himself out to the lost, poor, weak, blind, deaf, and lame. Whatever the need, John watched Jesus meet it.

John was also around when Jesus was whipped and beaten, spit upon and cursed. He was there when Jesus was spread out, nailed to, and then hung on a cross—Love in human form giving up His life for humanity. And John was there after the resurrection, when Jesus displayed His nail-scarred hands and feet. He witnessed Love ascend to heaven and experienced Love again when He descended in the form of the Holy Spirit. If anyone knew what Love was like, it was John.

And John, the guy who knew intimately what Love looked like and felt like and acted like, goes on to write about himself as "the *one* Jesus loved." As far as John was concerned, he was Jesus's favorite. Jesus loved him best.

Somehow John's relationship with Jesus nurtured the most profound revelation a person can possess. John knew God's love as an intimate, one-of-a-kind love. I believe that revelation is available to you and me.

To know I am "the *one* He loves" is my heart's truest desire, and I would like to suggest it's yours as well. Every day I am learning to believe Him when He says, "I love you." In fact, it's become my life's one true ambition, that I could say regarding myself, "I am the *one* He loves." And as I keep choosing to believe Him, I have come to realize it is the most important thing I will ever believe.

If I had only one opportunity to define the word *faith*, it would be this: "Faith believes God is love, His love is always good, and I exist to grow sure." Though I have but the smallest sliver of understanding, in my heart of hearts, where I continue to know His love in greater measure, I am betting I just might be His favorite; that He is especially fond of me, that He loves me best, that I am "the *one* He loves."

I'd also wager that if you ask Him, He will tell you the same thing.

The Puppy

Singing, oh my God, You are
Such a holy love, enough
And still I must have more

I was there with my four-year-old Ethan on the Virginia hilltop that crisp fall day. I sat on the trail edge with him in my lap, gazing out on the valley of blazing oranges and brilliant reds. And I prayed with him when he asked Jesus into his heart, when He experienced a revelation of Father, Son, and Holy Spirit. I was there when he discovered God is love, His love is always good, and He loved Ethan best. I was there when Ethan believed. It is one of my fondest memories.

Ethan isn't an overly expressive boy—except when scoring touchdowns. He is shy and quiet around strangers. I think it comes from his Canadian Anglo-Saxon roots. It's the same excuse I use for not dancing in public. For the two years following Ethan's salvation prayer, he was reserved. That is to say, his faith was a private one. When it came to life, he was loud at Lego Star Wars and flag football. But when it came to praying, he was beyond quiet—he had nothing to say.

It is safe to say that Ethan didn't like to pray. Not at the supper table, not at bedtime, not in the morning, "not in a box, not with a fox, not in a house, not with a mouse," and certainly not at church. He was shy. He was embarrassed. He did his best to give the impression of disinterest. I was facing a parent's tension. I wanted my son to learn how to pray, I knew as his dad it was my privilege to play catalyst, but I wasn't certain how to go about it. I had been trying to find a way to encourage him, not for form or religious expression, but for relationship—that he might encounter our Father's good love through prayer. I wanted his relationship to grow, for him to become sure. I wanted him to know the Promise Giver and discover his one-of-a-kind promise.

To embrace our promise, we must walk in close relationship with our Father, and one of the clearest ways this happens is through our prayer life, through discovering the gentle whisper of His voice in our hearts. I'm describing the daily opportunity to hear Him, to know Him, and to grow in revelation of who He is and His love for us.

Prayer is one of the ways we learn how to hear God when He speaks to our hearts—when He describes how He loves us. The Bible reveals we love because He first loved us (see 1 John 4:19). So if you think about it, prayer is less about talking and more about hearing Him. It is simply an invitation into a conversation He started before the foundations of the earth (see Eph. 1:1-4).

This hearing is absolutely essential to a life of faith, as Romans 10:17 says, *"Faith comes by hearing and hearing by the word of Christ"* (NASB). What that Scripture reveals is that faith, the gift of believing, is a current event. Faith is not available because you once heard God; it's the gift of daily, moment-by-moment communion with Him.

Imagine if our prayer life were actually the discovery of His voice speaking His perfect love over us. Imagine if our prayer life became a response to this revelation of who He is. Imagine how we would be transformed and launched into the one-of-a-kind greater works promise He has for us.

Prayer is a pretty big deal. I was intent on my son not just knowing the love of a good God on that Virginian hilltop, but also knowing the love of a good God at the Monday night family dinner table, or the Thursday afternoon school day, or the Saturday afternoon touchdown dance.

Several years ago on a Saturday morning, two years after Ethan's salvation experience, our kids came into the bedroom and jumped in bed with us. After the customary "good morning" and the "how did you sleep?" my daughter Maddy told a story about a friend of hers who just got a puppy.

As a parent of children without a puppy, this is dangerous territory. But before I could say anything to defuse the situation, Karen blurted out, "It sure would be fun to get a puppy!" That's all it took.

Maddy heard a positive comment about a dog, and the little fire we had spent years squelching immediately ignited into a raging inferno. "We should get one! I want a puppy *so* bad!" Ethan chimed in, "Me too! It would be so cool!" I looked at Karen incredulously and then did my best to give her the evil eye. She just smiled.

The rest of the morning was spent discussing all the reasons we couldn't get a dog right now. As I got out of bed I said, "Your sister Eva is too little." Maddy responded, "She's almost two, Dad, and then she will be three!" As I brushed my teeth, I garbled, "We don't have a fence." Maddy was ready for that one too: "I will walk him every day, three times a day!" she said. "Yeah, me too!" Ethan promised. As I put my shoes on to go for my morning run, I asked, "What about the poop—who's gonna pick it up?" I thought I had them, but Maddy didn't even hesitate, "We will, of course!"

When I returned from my run, Maddy and Ethan were waiting for me on the front porch. As I stretched, Maddy began explaining how they could get a bucket and a shovel and how her friend with the new dog picks up the poop with bags.

I showered, dressed, and found Maddy and Ethan waiting outside the bathroom door with drawings of them playing with the "beautiful puppy." "What's this one?" I asked Ethan. "In that picture I am wrestling with the puppy," he grinned. "And this one?" I asked as I took the second offering out of his hands. "In that picture I am sleeping with the puppy." He actually giggled, which if you are a parent you know is almost impossible to experience without joining in. I giggled with him and then realized I was dangerously close to being swayed by Maddy's sincere enthusiasm and Ethan's boyish charm.

I had to leave for a meeting. But before I left, I found Karen in her office and, with as much accusation as I could muster, said, "You started this!" She just smiled.

What I found when I got home blew my mind. Karen was on her computer, and the kids were hovering around her. As soon as I walked in, Maddy and Ethan started yelling, "Dad, come see, come see! It's the most cutest puppy ever!" "Seriously?" I said to Karen. She just smiled. The Maddy-Ethan-persistent-spouse stuff continued all afternoon and evening. And Karen just kept smiling.

Finally it was bedtime. I sat at the foot of Maddy's bed while she scratched my head, and Ethan sat on the floor with me. I told them a story about how, one time when I was younger, I went on a treasure hunt. I discovered a cave with a golden statue. The cave was booby trapped with poisonous arrows that shot out of the cave walls. And there was a huge pit I had to use my whip to swing across. And after I got the statue, the place started to cave in and a huge perfectly round boulder almost flattened me. I barely escaped the cave.

After my amazing and true story, which later I had to explain to my kids was made into a movie, I prayed for both of them. Maddy wanted to raise the puppy discussion again, but I pulled the old dad trick. "I don't want to talk about it anymore until I have discussed it with your mom." Then I herded Ethan into his bedroom to tuck him in.

When I got there, he didn't want to talk about the story or even wrestle. He just wanted to discuss the puppy. I had planned on using the same tactic I'd used with Maddy, when God's gentle whisper spoke to my heart. It was so beautiful I choked up. "Jason, I love you. Do you believe Me?"

Suddenly I knew what was on my Father's heart, and suddenly it was on my heart as well. While kneeling by Ethan's bed, I said, "Hey bud, let me ask you a serious question: how much do you think Father God loves you?"

He paused. "I don't know."

I asked another question. "Do you think God wants you to have a puppy?"

For a moment there was hope in his eyes. Then he got serious and again said, "I don't know."

I smiled and leaned in, "I want you to pray and ask Father whether we should get a puppy. You and He talk for a while and then you tell me what He says. We will do whatever He tells you."

I could barely control myself emotionally as I said this to him. I already knew my Father's answer. You see, He loves my son with a love that rivals His love for me. I kissed Ethan on the forehead and said, "I want you to really talk with God and hear what He says. When you have heard from Him, come tell me."

Ethan looked at me, scrunched his brow, and in a reverent tone said, "Okay, Dad."

About twenty minutes later he walked downstairs. "Dad?"

"Yes?" I said.

"I think God wants us to get a puppy." I nearly started crying again. My son was hearing his Father's voice—he was praying.

"Are you sure?" I asked.

"I think so." Ethan said.

"Well, I think so too, but I want you to be sure. Go pray some more until you are sure."

Another twenty minutes or so passed and he came down again, this time grinning ear to ear. "I'm sure, Dad!" he said.

"Me too. Let's get a puppy!"

A Greater Revelation

Your heart be our compass,
To be known by Your love

What would our lives look like if we could answer yes to the question our heavenly Father is always asking? What would happen if we believed He loved us perfectly and always? What would life be like if we could somehow live in a growing revelation that the plans He has for us really are always good? What kind of people would we become if we could somehow breathe in and out such authentic hope? How profound would our joy be to know this God?

First John 4:8 says it best: *"Whoever does not love does not know God, because God is love."* The words *God* and *love* are interchangeable. His very nature is Love. Every amazing attribute of God originates from Love, which means that the very foundation of this universe is Love.

What does Love look like? It looks exactly like Jesus. He is the perfect example of Love. But if we ever need a quick reference, we could read the famous wedding Scripture from 1 Corinthians 13 and replace the word *Love* with *God*, like this:

> *God is patient, God is kind. He does not envy, He does*
> *not boast, He is not proud. He is not rude, He is not self-*
> *seeking, He is not easily angered, He keeps no record of*
> *wrongs. God does not delight in evil but rejoices with the*

truth. He always protects, always trusts, always hopes, always perseveres (1 Corinthians 13:4-7).

When we begin to believe by faith that every God encounter is birthed from His perfect love, well, it changes everything else. Our ability to trust and live untamed, to engage our promise, is founded in believing He loves perfectly and "I am the one He loves." It's from this revelation that everything else flows. *Everything.*

I am convinced we exist for this revelation—to know His love that we might know more of His love. And the beauty of this revelation is that it transforms us and launches us into our promise. Principles and disciplines can be read about and discussed, they can be applied, but without revelation they carry no true power to transform. "God loves you" can be nothing more than words. But experiencing the words opens the door to the power of change.

God is love, and each time I say yes to His love, He reveals Himself to me in greater measure. I am learning that the more aware I am of how much He loves me, the greater access I have to the power of His love. I am learning that the power of His love is life altering. It's my salvation, my redemption, and my provision. It's my strength, my joy, and my peace. God's love is an all-consuming fire that encompasses every particle of me—*if* I surrender, *if* I let it. Every need or question I have is answered in a greater revelation of His always-good love.

I would like to suggest an untamed life begins when we believe He loves us. In fact, I'm convinced our promise is only embraced to the depth we believe God when He tells us He loves us.

This isn't a "feel-good gospel" I'm preaching; rather, this is a feel-good, love-good, live-good, die-good, pray-good, give-good, suffer-good, praise-good gospel…it's all good. This isn't name it and claim it, but this is about knowing and owning. This isn't about God giving us things, but about a greater revelation of His love meeting every need we may have, and more. This is about discovering He loves us as "the one," and regardless of our circumstances His love is good—always.

Our Prayer Life

All the laughter and wonder, breathed from our lungs
As Grace builds to thunder such a fiery love

Can you imagine if our hearts were like Ethan's when we prayed? Can you imagine if we could truly come to our Father with such sincere anticipation and then hear Him tell us how much He loves us? I believe if we knew His love, truly knew Him as Love, we would never fear again, sin wouldn't exist, and nothing would be impossible. Though this full revelation may not take place until we reach heaven, I believe it's available to us here, on earth, now, in greater measure than we could even ask or imagine.

I am discovering a prayer life centered on hearing and then agreeing with Him, a prayer life where all impossibilities become possibilities. Jesus modeled this prayer life perfectly. He was always "in the Father." He only did what He saw His Father doing and He only said what He heard His Father saying. His prayers were powerful—they healed the sick, set people free, and raised the dead. His prayers released the Kingdom of heaven on earth. This was because His prayers were responses to heavenly revelation—perfect love. They were simply agreement with heaven, with His Father's heart.

Prayer was never meant to be just a laundry list of needs. It's always been an invitation to a revelation of a perfect Love that meets *every* need. And I am discovering this revelation births such confidence. I am learning how to pray in the same confidence Jesus prayed, to pray in response to perfect Love, to pray as the *one* He loves. I am learning how to pray in the authority of my Father's agreement.

I believe Jesus's prayer life is promised to us. His example of intimacy, of walking in revelation, is available to us today. He promised greater works. The untamed life is the one where we learn to hear His voice, agree with Him, and lean into our greater works promise.

The Creator of the universe has written us into the greatest love story of all time. He has invited us to believe, engage His love, and *become* love with Him. He has invited us to hear His voice and experience the confidence that comes with knowing we are the *one* whom He loves. We are designed for revelation.

So when there was an economic meltdown and I asked Jesus if He wanted me to pray for financial breakthrough, He said, "Of course." When there was sickness and I asked if He wanted me to pray for healing, He said, "Always." And when I asked, "Jesus, do You want us to have a puppy?" "Yes," He said, and smiled.[1]

Endnote

1.   I believe every aspect of our faith revolves around our revelation of God's love. It's why this chapter is at the beginning of the book. It lays a firm foundation. Around 2009 God began to get very specific with me about His love. I was wrapping up the original version of this book and realized I wouldn't be able to put everything into this one chapter. So I handed the book in and continued writing toward that end. Over the next several years, I wrote and discovered His love in greater measure. In 2014 I released *Prone to Love* with Destiny Image. If this chapter spoke to your heart and you want to dive deeper into the revelation of His always-good love, *Prone to Love* is the next chapter in the story.

Chapter 3

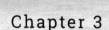

My Biggest Fear

I'm walking, waiting for You
Where is it You're going to
I trust we'll get there in time

Several years ago, my dad, my brother Joel, and I joined a pickup ice hockey league, which is better know as a beer league. This is a group of men who get to act like boys for a couple hours two nights a week. We loved it. It's the only time all three of us ever played together on the same team. One night, while Joel and I were resting on the bench, our dad took a shot to the head. Some nut on the other team actually threw a punch at him!

Joel and I were over the boards before you could blink, the natural instincts of both hockey players and sons making what happened next inescapable. Now this fella was big, and in all honesty could have taken us individually, but three on one, he didn't have a chance. Let's just say it's a good thing the other players were there or who knows what we would have done—"bad things, man…bad things."

After that incident, we became known as the Clark boys, and we were not to be messed with. The funny thing is that the Clark boys aren't really fighters. We are Canadian. That means we are nice. Yes, we may get a little rowdy at a hockey game now and then, but mostly we are nice.

I am originally from Canada, eh. This pretty much guarantees two other things besides being nice. One, I'm funny, but in an odd way, and two, I've loved and played the game of hockey since I took my first breath.

As a kid I existed to play hockey. During hockey season, I would often have very early games. I would fire out of bed well before the 5:30 a.m. alarm ready to play. I would check and double check to make sure my gear was all accounted for, my sticks taped and waxed. My dad would have to assure me over and over again that we were on time, he knew where we were going, my skates were sharp, and so on. I obsessed about being late. I didn't want to miss a moment.

When I was eighteen and graduating high school, I received the coveted invitation to tryouts. By then, I knew in my heart I wasn't skilled enough to make the NHL. I was also beginning to have different aspirations, which entailed melody and rhythm. But it took the devastation of getting cut in the third round to send me on another path. And just like that, my hockey career was over. It wasn't but a few years later that I started having the dream.

There were many variations of the dream but it always ended the same way. Sometimes in the dream I was a teenager, while at other times I was much younger. Regardless of my age, however, there was always a hockey game and there was always an obstacle to me being able to play.

In one scenario my dad and I would be on our way to the ice rink when something would happen to delay us, flat tires and traffic jams were common. We would arrive just as the game was ending. The stress was very real.

In another scenario we would get to the rink on time and I would begin to gear up only to find I had forgotten my laces, or my skates, or my stick, and I would have to watch the game from the bench while I waited for my dad to go home and get my gear.

Then there was the version where for no reason whatsoever, the coach simply wouldn't put me in the game. Last and worst was the dream where I would finally step out onto the ice just as it started melting and the ref would be forced to call the game. Whatever the scenario, there was one constant in every dream—I never got to play.

I would wake up angry, sometimes even in tears. The frustration of not getting to play would haunt me all day. Sometimes before going to sleep at night, I would visualize playing, determining I would play this time, but the dream always ended the same—I never got to play.

I had some version of this dream every five or six months over the course of ten years, well into my early years of marriage. Karen would wonder why I was restless on certain days and I'd tell her I had the dream again. The significance of these dreams did not occur to me until years after they stopped.

This dream unmasked one of my biggest fears in life—the fear that I would never get to play.

It still tries to haunt me at times—the idea that I will never be ready, or good enough, that I will forever sit on the bench, that the coach has no intentions of putting me in. I've lived much of my life scared that all the games will be played, all the songs written, all the revelation given to others. Scared I will spend my life watching others play the game I love, watching others revel in the thing I was born for. Scared I will never see the fullness of my promise. I'm being serious.

And I would guess I am not alone in these feelings.

American Idol

I'm walking, waiting for You…

I was watching *American Idol* awhile back. For obvious reasons, my favorite part of the show is the beginning of each season. I imagine it's like watching someone jump out of an airplane without a parachute. You don't want to see them bounce, but you just can't look away. So many of the contestants are desperate to be known; sadly, however, most of them can't sing and apparently have tone deafness or dishonest friends, or possibly both.

But this one particular story stirred my heart. A twenty-eight-year-old woman, at the top of the *American Idol* age limit that year, had put everything on the line to reach for her childhood dreams. She was married and had a little girl. She had pawned off her wedding ring for just enough money to get to DC for the auditions. Her husband wasn't totally on board, but he had come. And she was crying into the camera because if she didn't make the cut, she didn't know where they were going to sleep that night, as they were out of money.

Thankfully she could sing, and the judges, the infamous Simon included, passed her. When she came out for an interview, with tears in her eyes, she made a revealing and weighty statement to this effect: "Finally some validation. It doesn't matter if I win, I *can* sing." It seems she had waited most of her life for an accredited source to validate her ability, maybe even her identity. She had lived desperate for the words, "You are someone, you have a promise, you *can* sing."

It's almost as if for a moment the judges set her heart free from the haunting ghost, that ever-growing shadow of doubt regarding her promise. For a moment the judges had silenced the voices that daily whispered, "You can't, your dreams are foolish, you aren't worthy."

For her, the audition wasn't about winning a competition; it was about her promise. I think that's why she was crying—someone with "credentials" had recognized and therefore confirmed a part of who she believed she was but had never felt certain. And for at least a moment, she got to play, to be a contributor.

A couple days later I was sitting at lunch with a music artist, a worship leader, and successful pastor. It was like every lunch I'd had with worship leaders and pastors for the previous fifteen years. He talked and I was invisible. Seriously, for most of my adult life it's felt as if God Himself has hidden me. No matter what I said, the fella couldn't see me or recognize who I truly was.

I think we all have had this experience in some form or another; we all have been in the room and had some keen insight, some profound truth, some great passion, some powerful piece to add to the conversation, but no invitation or authority to give it away. To make matters even worse, it often feels like no one even knows we are in the room. It often feels as if we have been given a huge promise with an expiration date and are never invited to give it away. When we ask God about it, He kindly says, "Wait. Hold on. I got you. Trust Me. I see you." Over the early years of my life, I handled the waiting in many ways, occasionally with humility and grace but most often with frustration, insecurity, and fear…will I ever get to play?

I sat with this successful pastor quietly unsure. He was a little older and he was a "professional" musician and minister, after all. He had spent years becoming a "credentialed professional"—a fella with some titles. He probably even went to seminary. I had spent my years much the same way, except my pursuit didn't result in public affirmation. I was fighting insecurity and his security wasn't helping me one bit. I sat invisible, waiting for him to stop "preaching" at me. As if he had found all the most profound worship truths in the universe, as if I didn't already know them.

"Listen," I wanted to say, "that's great stuff you got there, but I just wanted to hang out and eat a sandwich. And maybe be seen as having something of worth to add to the conversation. I didn't sign up for a lecture."

So I got home from lunch and I started complaining to Karen. "This guy just doesn't see me. He treated me like I had just learned the earth wasn't flat. Can't he see that I'm just like him, I have a musical gifting and ability? Can't he recognize the heart I have for worship? Can't he recognize the promise God has given me? All we did was talk about him and what he knows. I know things too." If it sounds like I wasn't handling it with humility and grace, it's because I wasn't. If it sounds like I was whining, it's because I was. And if it sounds like I was searching for validation, yes, that too.

Karen reminded me, "Babe, you know what God has promised you. This guy doesn't have to see it for it to be true."

"I know, I know," I said. But Karen just didn't get it because, apparently, I did need him to see it.

I'm convinced one of the battles we face as believers is the one that rages between "being" and "being known." I believe our heavenly Father has placed a deep-seated desire within each of our hearts. We long to be known, to have our promise validated by "an accredited source." This is a holy longing, and while acknowledgement can ease the ache for a moment, only our Father can truly and fully satisfy it. We were designed to be known by Him and then to be known because of Him. He is the only true accredited source, the only One who can scratch the itch. Our validation, our identity, our promise is found in relationship with Him alone, and He loves us so much He will hide us until we discover and own this revelation.

Hidden

So remember me Jesus, here while I sing

Hiddenness is God's best for us. It is the gift of discovery. It's the invitation to trust in who He is so we can live sure in how He made us. The Bible is filled with stories of men and women who lived hidden for years before seeing the fullness of their promise. Jesus is the most profound example.

Jesus remained hidden for thirty years before the Father revealed Him to the world. How many "professional" sermons by "credentialed" leaders did Jesus listen to in obscurity? How many "accredited sources" taught from a pulpit while *God with Us* remained hidden in the audience? How many lunches did He sit invisible while listening to another person attempt an answer, when He was the answer?

Can you imagine knowing the answer to the question all of humanity is asking and having the grace and humility to wait until your Father says, "Okay, now is the time"? Jesus was perfectly content to be hidden within His Father's affection. His Father saw Him, loved Him and was well pleased with Him, and that was more than enough.

The Bible tells us that during those hidden years, *"Jesus grew in wisdom and stature, and in favor with God and men"* (Luke 2:52). I understand the wisdom and stature aspect of that verse, and I also understand how Jesus could grow in favor with man, but how and why would Jesus grow in favor with God? I think it had something to do with what Jesus was discovering while He was hidden.

At the age of thirty, John baptized Jesus in the Jordan River. His Father's voice thunders from heaven for all to hear: *"This is My Son, whom I love; with Him I am well pleased"* (Matt. 3:17). This moment launches Jesus into over three years of public ministry.

Jesus then reveals He is the greatest minister to ever grace the planet. But it dawned on me recently: Jesus was the greatest minister for the entirety of His life, not just the last three years of it. Yes, in those last years He revealed that perfect ministry looked like lots of miracles and powerful messages. But before that He revealed perfect ministry as living hidden in the pleasure of His Father. In the first thirty years, perfect ministry looked like growing in wisdom and favor with God…and then with man.

I believe Jesus was hidden for thirty years for one reason: to grow sure in His Father's love and discover His Father's pleasure. *"This is My Son, whom I love; with Him I am well pleased."* That's astounding! Jesus's hidden ministry pleased the Father. What if the favor of God is simply the discovery of His pleasure, and ministry is simply about growing more sure of it?

Jesus had the greatest promise of any man or woman who has ever walked the earth. In fact, He is *the* promise. And Jesus showed us how to live in and for the promise. It looked like thirty years of waiting and trusting and growing sure in the Father's pleasure.

Hiddenness is the beautiful gift of discovering our Father's love, His good pleasure. Obscurity is the preparation that invites us to know and trust Him. And I have learned this trust launches us into more beautiful opportunities to trust, to surrender to Him fully.

Stupid, Smelly Sheep

And if it's asked of me
To wait indefinitely
Then make my heart believe

I grew up in the church and therefore naturally developed a romantic view of the shepherd's life, as well as a fondness for sheep. You know, the children's storybook version, green rolling hills, sixty-eight degrees, slight breeze, soft fluffy sheep, and camping all the time—which means a campfire with roasted hot dogs and s'mores. On top of that, shepherds had adventures. For instance, David had the bear and the lion; and when Jesus was born, the angels sang to the shepherds who "watched their flocks by night." Jesus also talked of how much He loved the sheep, so you can understand—to me the shepherd's life was just short of perfect.

However, as I've grown, so has my perspective. I no longer want to live at a Taco Bell, be an astronaut, or play professional hockey—at least, most of the time. The shepherd's life has lost its appeal as well. It's hard work. There's rain, hours of boredom, and hundreds of smelly sheep—stupid, smelly sheep. No offense to you sheep enthusiasts, but in my opinion only the cow is worse when it comes to intelligence...or maybe our puppy. Did I mention we now have a puppy?

Samuel was famous in Israel; to meet him would have been equivalent today to meeting the Pope, only with less security. Not impressed? Okay, how about this. It would be like having Bono over for dinner. Samuel was the fella who ran things before the people of Israel demanded a king—the man who anointed Saul that king. He heard from God on behalf of a nation. So when he visited Jesse's house, filtered through all his sons, and pulled David out from the field and anointed him king, it was no little thing. It was a big deal. And then *the Spirit of God entered David like a rush of wind*" (1 Sam. 16:13 MSG).

I think when the promise became publically recognized, it was oddly familiar to David. I can't imagine he'd ever dreamed he would be king, but I believe he recognized the promise when he heard it. He had been carrying and nurturing the seed in his heart for years. Then suddenly he is introduced to his promise. He is validated by an "accredited source." And I bet that once it was spoken, everything made sense.

And then David goes back to tending sheep.

Have you ever experienced a time with God so profound, so holy, where for just a moment everything was clear and your journey made sense? Maybe it was when you were on your face in prayer, God was in the room, you felt His divine presence, and it was amazing. He spoke over you. He affirmed His promise and His love for you. Or maybe it was when someone else prayed for you and you sensed your destiny in his or her words. Or maybe it was simpler—you felt heaven's yes while listening to a song, reading a book, or watching a movie.

In that moment everything in the world fits together. Your past, present, and future are clear; your promise takes root in your heart. You know you are loved, you see God for the perfect Love He is, and you know who you are, and you make the decision to believe it. And then Monday morning comes and you go back to that job. Or maybe you lose that job. Or there is a family issue or an accident or even a death. Or your company fails, your marriage crashes, your health slips away.

Suddenly the promise seems no more than a distant memory, something beyond reality, too large to attain, maybe even foolish. Something tells me, for David, in one sense, tending sheep was easier, because now the promise had some definition and it had been publically recognized. But it also had to be tough, because even though the promise had been revealed and recognized, he was still "herding sheep."

I've been there—most of my life. And I think you know what I'm talking about. We all have a promise, a divine destiny, but it often seems after our Father confirms it we go right back to tending sheep. I would like to suggest how we choose to believe God during the "tending" makes a difference. Maybe all the difference.

Fringe

And if Your hand delays
On godly plans well made
Then give me eyes to see

"Shelved" is a music industry term. Record labels will generally sign a band or individual for a span of two to six years. They sign them with the intention of making and selling albums for a profit. But if for whatever reason it looks like the band won't make them money, they will "shelve" them, meaning the band and their album will never see the light of day as their album will not be released to stores. Trust me, it's a horrible experience if you're in the band.

As soon as I finished Bible college, I did what everyone expected. I started a band. Maybe that's not what *everyone* expected.

I believe there is such a thing as the perfect song for the perfect moment, a song so beautiful and right that to hear it would melt the hardest heart. A song so rock 'n' roll that a body is inspired and must move. A song so true that God and all of heaven join in the singing. I am convinced the perfect song in the perfect moment could bring healing to a broken world. I believe this because I have heard the perfect song in the perfect moment—it softened my heart, caused me to dream, believe, love, and hope, and it reminded me of who He is and who I am. I don't know that I've written the perfect song yet, but I'm still writing.

Music is in me. I was created for melody. So if you truly knew me, the band wouldn't have surprised you. I felt I had heard from God—He had given me words and Scriptures that encouraged me to believe I was meant to make music for Him, and I believed Fringe, the name of our band, was the means to that end. I am a singer and a songwriter, and for seven years my life revolved around the band. At the time, I was positive Fringe was the full expression of my promise.

For months, every other night of the week, we would practice until we finally felt we were good enough to play a show. We made a four-track recording and canvassed every bar and nightclub within a hundred miles. Then we went to open mic nights and battle of the bands until we began to line up gigs. More practice for the live album, which would be our first! Then back to the street to line up more gigs, more practice, and countless hours writing songs. We played pretty much anywhere that would let us. It didn't matter whether there were 10 people or 200—we played with everything we had. And the years passed.

Then we made our first studio record—a tribute to every independent band out there. We shopped it to every label under the sun. The Kinko's staff knew us by name—we practically lived there since that was the best place to put together press kits. We made hundreds of them. Then mail-out after mail-out, every record label got one. And then rejection letter after rejection letter until the day all bands covet—the phone call from a label. We were signed. More practice, more shows, and new bandmates. And more years passed by.

Finally the big payoff came. We signed a six-year deal with another label—this label had both money and connections! More practice and new songs for the new big-budget album with Grammy award-winning engineers and producers. Months in the studio, oh the beautiful process of recording an album with a real budget. Then mixing, photo shoots, magazine interviews, and bigger and better shows. Then the radio interviews as the single was released. The CD was packaged and sent out to magazines for reviews. The reviews started to come in:

> Trailing flashes of brilliance, traces of Matthews and U2's influence, but mostly just great and greatly produced songs of humble strength and unique sound. Fringe paints in the colors of wonder. This group is on top of the pile.[1]

And

> Clark's vocals have a richness, a fullness, surrounded with a harmony that borders on symphonic.[2]

And

> The lyrics are poetic, understated and intimately delivered. The band offers hope for the broken...imagine worship without the cliché, just the honesty.[3]

We had done it. All the hard work had finally paid off. Thank You, God! I was finally getting to live my promise!

And then we heard the news. The label had lost their distribution. The album wasn't going to be released—it would not be made available for sale. The album was "shelved," but the label, due to their investment, decided to pick up the option in our contract. This meant we were contractually obligated to the label and couldn't make another album for four years. A band makes most of their income off of album sales from live shows, which means albums are a band's lifeblood.

It was over. And that's the story of my band.

The Wilderness

I'm walking, waiting for You...

We were "shelved"—it was over and I couldn't believe it. My whole adult life had been given to the band. All those hockey dreams of me never getting to play came crashing home. I was miserable. One moment I was chasing down my promise with passion and the next I had been dragged into the wilderness, that place of disappointment, sorrow, and pain, where time itself seems to have forgotten you. Fully and completely hidden.

The next several years I lived in a spiritual wasteland much like the famed wilderness in the Bible where the Israelites spent forty years just hanging out waiting to die. God was there with manna and water but not much else.

Before this season, I used to dread the idea of the wilderness; it was something to be avoided at all costs. But over the course of several years, I came to understand if we breathe for long enough we will experience wilderness seasons in life. Whether it's the loss of a loved one, a career derailed, or just a season of waiting, it's usually something we have little to no control over. What's crazy is the wilderness season often comes right on the heels of receiving the promise.

I think many of us have experienced this phenomenon. We receive God's promise and then get "shelved." It's nothing new. If you look at the heroes in the Bible, most of them spent years hidden on the shelf. Joseph, Moses, David—they all spent time "herding sheep" after the promise of God had been established in their hearts. They all did time in the wilderness.

Jesus Himself modeled this for us too. After His baptism, after His Father shook the heavens with a voice like thunder declaring His love and pleasure, after the Holy Spirit descended in the form of a dove and rested upon Him, Jesus walks into a wilderness. I would have expected Him to step out of the water and begin His signs and wonders, find men to disciple and miracles to do. Instead, Jesus steps out of the water, follows the Holy Spirit into a wasteland, and models for us what it looks like to embrace our promise.

What is most amazing about this story is that it was the Father who led Jesus into the wilderness. The Bible tells us Jesus did nothing apart from His heavenly Father. He lived out the perfect will of God. Jesus willingly surrendered to hiddenness, whether it was the complete obscurity before His baptism or the willingness to surrender to the wilderness directly after. He modeled trust in His Father's love. He revealed what it looked like to fully embrace His promise by continually surrendering it into His Father's hands.

I spent the first twenty years of my life learning about my unique promise and the last twenty learning how to surrender that same promise. I'm learning the extent to which I possess my promise is directly linked to the measure of my surrender. Strangely, to truly participate in my promise now, I must surrender it and discover absolute dependence in the Promise Giver. And that's where the wilderness comes into play.

It's the wilderness that prepares our hearts. In the wilderness we learn to surrender our understanding of the promise. And in this surrender, we begin to see our promise through our Father's eyes. This is absolutely essential if we want to fully embrace our promise.

I now believe the wilderness is the place where our relationship with our Father can be developed. This is a place where He can daily meet with us and provide for our needs, where He can stretch and increase our capacity to believe with Him. Even in the midst of disappointment, sorrow, or pain, the wilderness can become a place of trust, beauty, and surrender. It can become a place where we believe even when He seems distant, we can grow sure in His love, His grace, His kindness, and His goodness. It's one of the places where our Father can deepen our revelation of who He is in connection to where He wants to take us.

The wilderness is also the season of life where we have the opportunity to become sure in our identity as a son or daughter. "This is My Son." That was the last thing Jesus heard from His Father before going into the wilderness. "If you are the Son of God" was the first thing the enemy used against Jesus when he came to tempt Him.

The enemy of our promise will attack us in one of two ways. First, he will endeavor to undermine our trust in the good love of our Father, and second, he will endeavor to undermine our confidence in our identity as a beloved son or daughter. The wilderness is the place where we develop faith—faith that our Father is good regardless of what we are experiencing, and faith that we are His favorite, His child, the one He loves regardless of our bleak circumstances.

I wonder if we were to go straight to the promise without the wilderness, would we believe enough to live out the promise or would it destroy us?

However, we must remember the wilderness is not our home. It is not our promise. It is not the end of the story. I know from experience if believing wanes in the wilderness, if we lose track of who

He is and whose we are, then we will begin to settle there, thinking, "This must be as good as it gets."

I'm afraid many Christians in wilderness seasons have stopped believing and taken up permanent residence, mistaking the wilderness as the Promised Land. There is nothing wrong with wilderness living as long as we understand it is not our promise. It was never meant to become our home. There is so much more. We cannot settle there.

Bathtubs or Oceans

I stood on the edge to see what I could see
Told my heart to never forget Your Spirit birthed in me

When Eva was two, we went on a beach vacation. Weeks before the trip, the whole family told her about the ocean. "It's the biggest swimming pool ever!" Maddy informed her. "The waves are awesome!" Ethan explained. The entire drive to the coast, we regaled her with tales of the sea. She was primed for big water.

After checking into the twenty-five-story beachfront condo, we immediately went out onto our balcony eighteen stories up to finally show Eva the unending body of water. Her eyes took it in and she finally understood. The ocean is *big*.

If you have been on a beach vacation with small children, then you know it can easily take an hour from the moment you decide to go swimming to the moment you actually leave the condo. Especially if you have Anglo-Saxon skin. The process seems endless: putting on bathing suits, gathering boogie boards, collecting towels, selecting beach toys, packing the cooler, and lathering sunscreen on in generous amounts upon every surface that could even possibly see a moment of sun and a few spots that shouldn't, just in case. Along the way, the kids become almost unbearable. Their understanding of "be patient" is waiting three minutes between asking, "When are we going to the beach?"

While we prepared, Eva got caught up in her older brother and sister's euphoric expectation. The kids would run to the balcony and look at the "osen," as Eva called it, and laugh. Then Ethan would exclaim he was going to ride the biggest wave on his boogie board which he carried everywhere. Then they would come find us to ask, "Aren't we ready yet?" and "Can we go now?"

Waiting is so hard.

Finally, everyone lathered in sunscreen, towels accounted for, flip-flops on, we headed for the door. I did a head count and found that Eva was not among us. I called for her. "Eva, let's go swim in the osen! Eva?" There was no response. I walked through the condo and finally found her naked in the master bathroom trying to get into the tub. "What are you doing?" I asked.

"Mmm, take a baff, Daddy," she said.

"What about the ocean?"

My daughter, tired of waiting, and upon seeing the bathtub, forgot about the ocean. She was more than willing to trade the ocean she had not experienced for the familiarity of the tub.

Suddenly my Father spoke to my heart and said, "Jason, the promises I have for you are the size of the ocean. Don't get distracted by bathtubs."

The moral of this story? Not all water is created equal. Your promise, my promise—it's huge! It's as big as the ocean. We must live expectant, hopeful, patiently believing. We can't afford to lose sight of it or we will be tempted to settle for bathtubs.

Embracing Our Promise

There is a freedom found in surrender
My sacrifice, my song to You

In Matthew 5:14 Jesus says, *"If I make you light-bearers, you don't think I'm going to hide you under a bucket, do you? I'm putting you on a light stand"* (MSG). I'm convinced our Father wants to show us off for the whole world to see. He wants to show us off for His glory. But when the recognition comes, it will be a by-product of God's recognition.

Jesus did nothing apart from His Father. He waited until He was thirty before being released into His public ministry. He surrendered Himself to the wilderness and later to the cross. He was always patient, never forcing the Holy Spirit. He perfectly walked out the fulfillment of His promise, and everything He did glorified His Father. He had no agenda higher than that, and He fully embraced His promise from His first breath to His ascension.

Insecurity haunts humankind, a holy insecurity or void, and only Father God can fill it. I cannot allow my worth to be determined by the eyes of "accredited sources." My promise is not defined by the applause of peers. My promise is embraced through surrender. It's found through the hidden seasons and in the obscurity of a wilderness where my focus and trust shifts from me to Him.

Whether we are called to Hollywood or Haiti, it's our surrender that defines us. It's our Father's intention that we all get to play. There are no benchwarmer promises in His Kingdom. God is the One who created this game and He gave us the passion and ability to play it.

I believe He is teaching us how to live bigger, how to discover a greater works life. And to live bigger we have to be intimate with surrender, absolute dependence. Embracing the promise is about surrendering it back to Him and allowing Him to define it and fulfill it in His timing and not forcing ours. It's showing patience, standing firm, and believing in the face of devastating heartache and incredible obstacles. Embracing the promise could look like waiting, hiddenness, long-suffering, the wilderness and even death. But embracing the promise is the only way to truly be alive.

Endnotes

1. Gary Hassig, CBA Marketplace.

2. Kristine Brown, Diganote.

3. Mark Fisher, 1340 Magazine.

Chapter 4

The Believe Switch

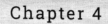

The Audible Voice

Made good on grace, surrendered to the winds
Up and away, the life I was born to live

Note: I have changed the names in the following story because it's much funnier…and because my sister told me to.

Have you ever heard the audible voice of God? I mean the actual audible voice? On a daily basis I encounter God through reading, prayer, and, of course, through music. Throughout the day, He speaks to me and I am learning how to hear Him on a more regular basis. And then there have been the profound, unmistakable meetings with God where I've experienced the power of His presence in my heart, soul, mind, and strength.

There was one time I heard Him speak to me audibly. It's only happened once, and this is what He said: "You're kissing another man's wife."

When I was ten years old, the kids in my class started to tease me about Wonder Woman (name changed). There was a song they loved to sing when Wonder Woman and I were in the same room. It went something like this: "Jason and Wonder Woman sitting in a tree / K-I-S-S-I-N-G / First comes love, then comes marriage / then comes a baby in the baby carriage." It's a catchy tune—it really gets in your head.

The song didn't bother me much; I was only slightly embarrassed. But more than anything, I was surprised. In my ten-year-old mind, it made sense we were in a tree, but in all honesty I hadn't given much thought to the love part yet. But the kids kept singing the song and Wonder Woman seemed nice, so I started considering it. Ten children seemed about right—I even came up with a few names like Talon, Blade, and Lightning…and, of course, Thunder. And as far as the kissing was concerned, did we really have to?

One night my dad overheard my sister, Aimee, and I talking about the impending nuptials. He called me over. "Jason, you are too young to be thinking about girls," he said. And that was that. The wedding was called off and I stopped thinking about Wonder Woman and our ten kids. When I was young, many things were just easier. If Dad said, "Don't worry about it," well, then I stopped worrying about it.

However, three years later I met Princess Leah (name changed again). She was my sister's best friend (now you can see why my sister wanted me to change names). I liked her and I didn't need anyone singing songs about baby carriages to be convinced. She was pretty and nice and, well, I don't think my dad could have talked me out of this one. Smitten, that's the word.

For months Aimee, Princess Leah, my friend Fonzie (yeah, Fonzie), and I would hang out. Our favorite place was the mall, and between the mall and youth group, Leah and I developed a friendship that would make you giggle.

Then one night our youth group had a cookout at a farm that belonged to a church member. It was one of those magical nights with a bonfire, a hayride, caramel apples, and, of course, the Princess. Leah smelled nice and she laughed at my jokes and at one point we began to hold hands. It was intoxicating.

Late in the evening, we all went for a walk. Somewhere along the way, Aimee and Fonzie lagged behind, and suddenly I was alone with Leah. I could hear the Tiffany song in my head, "I think we're alone now / there doesn't seem to be any one a-rah-hound / I think we're alone now / the beating of my heart is the only sa-ound...." I was holding her hand and I could barely breathe. Before I could think of anything to say or do, she kissed my cheek, then turned and ran back to the bonfire, laughing.

About four months later, my family moved to the Northwest and Princess Leah's family moved to Indiana. But Leah and Aimee stayed in touch, and over the years the Princess and I would write each other and occasionally talk on the phone. I never forgot that kiss, and so when she came out to visit us one summer, we picked up right where we left off. At the age of seventeen, Princess Leah officially became my girlfriend, and at the age of eighteen, I left home for a job.

This job allowed me to travel through Indiana on a regular basis. As Princess Leah lived with her parents, whenever I came through I would stay at her house and we would go on a date. Love—true love. I wrote her a beautiful song about climbing mountains and swimming oceans just to see her. Imagine that Bryan Adams song from Kevin Costner's *Robin Hood* and you pretty much got it. It made her cry.

When I wasn't with her, I would spend hours writing her letters and dreaming about what life would be like with her. In fact, there were no future scenarios without her. In my mind we were married with kids, already pros at the K-I-S-S-I-N-G.

One night while I was praying, I realized I had given an awful lot of my heart to Princess Leah and hadn't even considered inviting

God into my fantasy. I began to converse with my heavenly Father, and as I did He pointed out how I had gone pretty far down the road of my future without inviting Him into any of the decisions I had made. Then He asked me if He or Princess Leah was first in my life. When I realized I couldn't answer that question correctly, I became frustrated and depressed.

Over the next month I agonized in my prayer life as my Father kept gently bringing that question back to my heart. Finally I said, "Okay, Father, I want to put You first, but I really like Princess Leah. What's a man to do?" I felt like God asked me to take a break. I was frustrated and yet I trusted Him and His love for me. And so in my heart I determined that the next time I saw Leah, I would obey God and put our relationship on hold. The next time I saw her ended up being the following week.

I arrived in the afternoon and spent a few hours with her family before taking her out on a dinner date. I planned on breaking the news over dinner, but the way she looked at me got me worrying about her feelings. I knew she loved God and I felt she would not only understand but would also probably be quite impressed with my godliness. Still, I decided to wait and tell her after dinner. "Maybe in the car," I thought.

After dinner we drove around until eventually we found a church parking lot. It was a true country church—in the middle of a field in the middle of nowhere. I planned on telling her during the drive, but she was holding my hand. When we parked, I turned on the tape deck—U2's "I Still Haven't Found What I'm Looking For." I rolled down the windows and we took a blanket and sat on the hood of the car. "Okay, Father, I'll tell her now," I thought. Then I kissed her.

And then I heard it. I kid you not. In an audible voice, God said, "You are kissing another man's wife!" It was so loud and so strong that I jerked back from Princess Leah. I looked at her to see if she had heard it, but she simply looked confused; apparently she hadn't heard anything. But I had. I was so shaken up, not just by my failure to obey God but also by the message. Princess Leah wasn't mine. Bono cooed in the background, "I still haven't found what I'm looking for...."

Princess Leah married a nice fella a year or two later. That seems long ago now, in a galaxy far away.

God's plans for our lives are so much grander than ours, His thoughts always surpass our thoughts, and His dreams are bigger and better than we could ask for or even imagine. His goodness is beyond our comprehension. I learned this firsthand a year later when, at Bible college, I met my wife-to-be, my Karen. No one is more perfect than she is. And my Father knew this. He saw my future and said, "It is good!" On top of all of that, I *get* to kiss her! We have three perfect kids with really cool names, and that's better than any man could hope for. As Bono says, she's "the real things, even better than the real thing."

Our Father has a promise for each and every one of us. He is never caught off guard or surprised, and if we say yes to Him, if we are willing to trust and obey Him, He will work it in us and for our good. I have learned He doesn't always tell us *why*. He rarely gives us the whole picture or interpretation, He rarely speaks out loud, but He will be sure to guide us—He can be trusted.

I have also come to discover God's timing is better than mine. I can push my own agendas or I can rest and keep my eyes fixed on Him. It's my responsibility to follow, trust and obey and His pleasure to redeem, restore, and work all things to my good. In my prayer time, my Father was gently telling me He had something else, something perfect for me. However, I was so blinded by my idea of what my future could look like that I wasn't able to fully surrender. I can't tell you how many stories I have like this in my life. Stories where my best idea of my future blinded me to His best idea of my future.

I have grand promises from God, yet oddly enough I often have had a hard time along the way trusting Him to bring them to fruition. I've often gotten an idea and found myself mid-chase before discussing it with Him. I have tracked things down and made things happen. I'm innovative—I can almost always make it work. I can almost always make something fit. But thankfully my Father in His mercy and grace has stepped in every time and said, "Jason, this isn't My best for you," or "No, this isn't My plan, it's yours." Then there was the time He said, "Hey, you are kissing another man's wife!"

Sometimes I think I know the best ending to my story even though at the age of five I asked Jesus to be the Author and perfecter of it. But I am learning even when my Father leads me to a place that seems contrary to everything I understand, in the end I know His characters always get the "girl." The question is, what do I believe about God? Is He good, is His love perfect, and can I surrender to Him? The answer to those questions will either empower radical obedience and transformative trust or a prodigal heart.

Giving It Back

I've said You're the Son of God and I've forced water from a stone
And I've searched my heart's ruins till Your heart was found

I was standing near the back of the concert hall at a Delirious show, watching the band lead a few thousand people into a rock 'n' roll worship experience. It was about eight months since my band Fringe had ceased to exist. I was miserable. There I was watching a group of guys do what I had chased after for seven long years. It felt like they were living my promise. They were up there doing what I was created to do. I felt like God had discarded me. The word *fringe* took on a whole new meaning.

Karen and I left the show early. On the drive home she started talking about the concert, about the kids, and about life in general.

After a short time she realized I was so emotionally exhausted that if I opened my mouth I would no doubt fall apart. She sensed my pain, so she took my hand in hers and we drove the rest of the way home in silence. When we walked in the door, I didn't even acknowledge the babysitter. I walked past her to our bedroom and into the bathroom—it was the only place I was sure to be alone. I collapsed onto the floor.

I remember lying there, crying out to my Father my absolute sadness as the ghost of my promise tortured me with my failures. For so long I had been haunted by my promise of music. But that dream was over, that night the music died, and I just couldn't understand it. I remember telling my Father it felt as if He had made me into a hammer and then kept asking me to cut something. I often think in analogies, and this was the best one I could come up with for what I was feeling at that moment. Why give me a promise if there was no intention of fulfilling it?

I had spent seven years keeping the vision alive, kicking and scratching and clawing and pulling and working and sweating and grinding out a future in music because that's where my promise was. That's what you have to do when God gives you a promise, right? In the end, I had failed and I was utterly heartbroken and exhausted.

That night I had a decision to make. I didn't know I had a decision at the time, but by the grace of God I made the right one. That night, after hours of crying out to God, I found myself at the difficult and beautiful place known as the cross. That night I surrendered my promise back to God. "Not my will but Yours," I prayed.

Though I didn't see the fullness of it at the time, looking back, that was the moment I began living my promise, the moment I fully embraced it. That was the moment I made a shift from unbelief to believing. The next morning, with absolutely no agendas, I went up to my music room and wrote a song. Some of the lyrics go like this:

> *Come, let's go up to the mountain.*
> *Come, let's worship 'neath the cross.*
>
> *Come, let's know our Savior's journey and*
> *find our story in His song.*

Once you experience a revelation in your heart, it takes some time to walk it out. That is to say, my heart was changed but my life did not immediately reflect that change. I had to begin to make the transition in my thinking and in my actions.

The next few years I experienced a radical renewing of my mind (see Rom. 12:1-2). God began changing the way I think and that began to affect everything. Everything practical, emotional, and spiritual began to be viewed through the heart of my Father and His love. I made a decision to lay everything down, and in so doing I made a decision to believe.

The Believe Switch

Faith is not the absence of doubt: it's the presence of belief.
I may not always feel that I have great faith. But I can always obey[1]

Just because you make the decision to believe doesn't mean life suddenly hands you unicorns and rainbows. You may ask, "How does one believe?" I mean, there isn't a believe switch that you can suddenly turn on. You either do or you don't.

I struggled with day-to-day believing. I was shocked by my cynicism and by how much unbelief I had lived with. This ugly thing known as realism seemed to be how I approached almost every aspect of life. Somehow, I had become a saved unbeliever, and I was determined to change that. I had only one prayer throughout this season: "God, help me believe."

One Mississippi summer day, after working eight hours on a roof in the 98-degree heat, I asked my Father with sweaty sincerity, "Do You have a believe switch? If You've got one, I would sure like to know what it looks like and where to locate it." He responded to my heart by saying, "I've got one—it's called obedience, your surrender and discovery of My good and perfect will. You're doing great! I'm proud of you and you are the *one* I love!"

And so I began a journey, an intentional step-by-step surrender to the good and perfect will of God. Whenever there was a choice, I chose to obey—to believe He was good and that my promise was secure in Him. And in so doing, I chose to trust. As the days turned to months, I began to notice the ghost of my promise wasn't haunting me as strongly as it always had. I began to realize, even though my circumstances didn't change and certainly didn't appear to be relevant to my promise, that I was becoming a believer.

Here is what I am learning: obedience births believing. And what's amazing about this is that if you practice obedience enough, believing becomes part of who you are. I really think this is what Paul was talking about when he wrote about the renewed mind. The Scripture says, *"Do not conform any longer to the pattern of this world, but be transformed by the renewing of your mind. Then you will be able to test and approve what God's will is—His good, pleasing and perfect will"* (Rom. 12:2). The mind is renewed through a believing heart, and the believing heart is birthed in surrendered obedience where we discover He is trustworthy and so good.

I want a renewed mind, because with it I can hear and know the heartbeat of my Father. With a renewed mind I can know all God's desires, and His desires can become mine. I am convinced that's how to truly embrace my promise.

Obedience

I came believing with righteous intent
To lay hold of innocence

When my kids were younger, they didn't need deep revelation on why obedience was important, but I did. I wasn't interested in disciplining them unless I could understand why. Was it so they would become respectable contributing members of society, or was it so they could understand the value of rules? Was it so they could be well-rounded, civilized, and safe?

I've always made my love known while disciplining my kids. And rarely am I upset—well, there was that time I lost my cool because my two-year-old thought poop made good art. Karen and I are still not quite sure what he was drawing on his bedroom wall, but I'd put my money on a spaceship. "You don't play with your poop," I kept saying, until Karen kindly asked me to leave. Really, I was just shocked it was something that had to be taught.

When I discipline my kids, there is always the explanation of "you have to learn how to obey." But why is obedience so important? In the Book of Acts, Paul and his entourage are out preaching the gospel, and one day Paul says, "I feel compelled by the Holy Spirit to go back to Jerusalem. I'm not sure what is going to happen, but I'm pretty sure it won't be easy. In fact, the Holy Spirit has made it clear there are hard times ahead" (see Acts 20:22-24).

When those around Paul heard this, they begged him not to go. Yet from town to town Paul ignores their pleas and continues on. When he reaches the town of Ptolemais, he meets with a prophet. This fella had come some distance with a word from the Holy Spirit. With great showmanship the prophet lets Paul know that if he continues on to Jerusalem, he will be tied hand and foot. More or less, Paul was headed for a jail cell or worse.

God was speaking. The people who loved Paul heard Him, and even the prophet heard Him. But their interpretation of God's message was missing a key element. God had asked Paul to go to Jerusalem. He was simply obeying what God had already revealed to him. This is what Paul had to say about it:

> *Why do you insist on making a scene and making it even harder on me? You're looking at this backward. The issue in Jerusalem is not what they do to me, whether arrest or murder, but what the Master Jesus does through my obedience* (Acts 21:13-14 MSG).

God often asks of us things that land clearly outside of human reasoning. In fact, they appear foolish. But Paul had experienced God in such profound ways that his thinking had been transformed and everything he did was now filtered through an eternal Kingdom perspective. He understood that obedience was the faith of a mustard seed in action, and because God said go to Jerusalem there was nothing he could do that would be better for him or have a greater impact on the world. You know, many of the books in the New Testament are there because of Paul's obedience to God.

It is because I love my kids that I must teach them about the importance of obedience. Our Father's best for them is discovered in their obedience. He has astounding things He wants to do with them, and the better understanding they have regarding obedience, the greater they can know Him and grow in trust and faith. It's faith that moves mountains, and God desires to move mountains with my kids—they were born for greatness.

Obedience is the response of a heart that knows love. Obedience is surrender; it's the doorway to fulfillment and the key to living wild. It's this kind of obedience that defines world changers. Oswald Chambers put it this way: "The promises of God are of no value to us until, through obedience, we come to understand the nature of

God."[2] It is in obedience that we grow in His love and it is in obedience that He finds us trustworthy with the deeper longings of His heart. Obedience is what lands us in the best stories, the ones where we get to experience overwhelming circumstances, and then we get to discover His wonderful faithfulness.

Obedience is an amazing thing. The more we obey, the more opportunities God has to reveal Himself and His promises. Paul wrote, *"All the promises of God in Him are Yes, and in Him Amen"* (2 Cor. 1:20 NKJV). A yes born from obedience will reveal and empower His promises in our lives.

Past Comfortable

I believe it's begun and is finished, a revolution of the cross
I've awakened to a movement, love my burden, the birthplace of
holiness

When it comes to embracing our promise, our biggest enemy is comfort. Don't get me wrong: when it's time to sleep, I want my king-size bed and my beautiful Karen to scratch my head. And I must have a fan—not because I'm hot, but for the noise. I can't have wind blowing on me because it dries out my throat. The sheets have to be at least 400 thread count and…well, you get the point. I like comfort and…I'm a princess.

While it's perfectly fine to enjoy the wonders of down comforters, we will not fully embrace our promise unless we're willing to step into uncomfortable radical obedience. God will often invite us into uncomfortable situations in order to reveal His love—He will ask for crazy seemingly foolish obedience and reveal He is trustworthy. He will say something like "Come to Me" while He is standing on water in the middle of a raging storm. But here is the thing—if we trust and obey, we get to walk on water.

What I've begun to realize is that though I want to see God move miraculously, I rarely allow myself to be in a situation where I need a miracle. Though I desire to live an untamed faith, I am rarely willing to position myself in discomfort. Years ago I decided I couldn't define success by how comfortable I am. There must always be something in my life I believe for, something that's bigger than me, bigger than my abilities and resources. There must always be a place in my life where I'm living in expectation of the impossible bending its knee, a place where the miracle is my answer, a place of full surrender and total dependence.

And I am discovering my promise like never before.

I'm growing more sure when it comes to living in the miraculous. I am hungry for my Father's presence, so I'm simply saying yes. Yes to obedience and yes to engaging my promise and yes to advancing the Kingdom through a greater works life.

Endnotes

1. Bill Johnson, *When Heaven Invades Earth,* (Shippensburg, PA: Destiny Image Publishers, 2005)

2. Oswald Chambers, *My Utmost For His Highest.*

Chapter 5

Do It for the Story

A Family Story

I come from a family of storytellers. My brothers Joel is a film-maker and author. He has written several books, including a brilliant fantasy series for young adults entitled Jack Staples. My sister, Aimee, has written a children's book entitled *Free as a Leelee Bird*—it's about the wonder of forgiveness and it is amazing. My dad, Lloyd, has nearly finished his memoir; it's a humorous and heart-transforming journey into Perfect Love. But long before we ever thought to film or write our stories, we were telling them over the dinner table.

When we all get together, it can be loud. Our family dinner table is often rowdy. We love to laugh and reminisce—"Oh, man, do you remember when…"—the mischievous memories and the daring, dangerous tales are favorites. We love to hear about what God is doing in our lives today—"You've got to be kidding!" and "Wow, doesn't God love us!" are classic responses. Our absolute, hands-down favorites are the wild God stories, His promises coming to life. We just love the stories of untamed trust, where miracles happened.

These stories remind us of who He is and they always cause us to dream into the future with wild expectation.

My family wholeheartedly believes that *story* is the best way to communicate the goodness of God. We live to discover the greater works story, the family story our heavenly Father is always revealing. And we are also passionate about telling the story. But you can't give away what you don't have. To tell a good story you have to live a good story. And to live a good story you have to be willing to *do it for the story.*

Do It for the Story

It's time to change the world
To live life true and wild,
My revolution of my heart

Years ago, long before we filmed or wrote our stories, my brother Joel told me that when he was eighteen he came up with a life theme or motto: do it for the story. At first, I thought Joel's theme was a little irresponsible. I mean, a life theme should be something more Mother Teresa-ish, like "Lay down your life for the poor, sick, and oppressed, the widow and the orphan." Shouldn't it? Over the years, as I have discovered the Promise Giver, I've come to believe my brother knew what he was talking about. As I have grown sure in God's love, I've realized it's simply brilliant. Yes, do it for the story—His story and yours.

The best story, the one we truly desire to live, is found in His story. Jesus's story is the one where we see our heavenly Father and are transformed by His love. His story reveals the Promise Giver and our promise. It birthed a revolution that's changing the world. It was dangerous and looked foolish and required trust and led to death and then glorious resurrection. When His story is embraced, our story becomes beautiful, powerful, transformative, and full. When His story is embraced, we are invited to do it for our own story!

Mother Teresa did it for the story and discovered her promise. The poor, the sick, the oppressed, the widow, and the orphan were powerfully loved. Hers was an uncomfortable, foolish, surrendered, untamed, beautiful, and powerfully transformative story.

I'm in hot pursuit of untamed God stories. I have moved and stayed for them, literally and figuratively. I will go halfway around the world for them. I once shared with a group of believers in the Philippines that I had come in search of stories—God's, theirs, and mine.

How do we find untamed God stories? It's simple: when God invites us to step out, when He invites us to obey, to trust, to pray for that person, to give when it's uncomfortable, to try something new and maybe a little dangerous or foolish, when He invites us to trust even when it might seem crazy, or when it's risky and we might fail, we say yes.

Yes. It's a simple but powerful heart position that introduces us to the most powerful and transformative stories. This life with God was never meant to be a theory or a set of principles. We were created for experience—to taste and touch, to search and discover. Why else does a thirteen-month-old experience such joy in the discovery of a light switch or bubbles? Okay, I get bubbles. But why do I come alive at the top of a mountain? And why did God invite Adam to name the animals? God created them, so one would naturally think He's the One best suited to name them. Yet from the beginning, God set up the universe with all of its wonders and mysteries for our discovery, for our pleasure, for our experience, for our story.

Our relationship with Him works much the same way. We have been invited to discover His heart until we begin to see, hear, and feel as He does, until we begin to collect our own crazy, foolish, amazing, untamed, miraculous stories, the ones we share with our family at the dinner table, the stories in which we grow more sure in our promises. We have been invited to do it for the story—our story and His.

Foolish and Crazy

I saw the burning bush
I went to take a look
You were there

Many years ago I was sitting at a table outside of Starbucks in an outdoor shopping plaza. I was quietly writing this book and planned on meeting Karen and the kids a little later for some ice cream and shopping. I was enjoying a caramel macchiato when I recognized a fella walking by. He had recently spoken at our church and told some amazing God stories. Before long we were sitting around the table, being a little loud, possibly even rowdy.

He began to share with me some of his crazy cool God stories, the kind of stories I want more of, stories of deaf people hearing, blind people seeing, lost people becoming found. After a sweet time of fellowship, and after my heart had been expanded, and after I had started dreaming of the future with wild expectation, Karen and the kids arrived. I said good-bye, thanking him for his stories, and we went family shopping.

Maddy had $5.00 burning a hole in her pocket and we found a Pottery Barn for kids, or something like that. I was drunk with anticipation and love for Jesus. The miracle stories had stirred my hunger for more of my own crazy stories. That's what happens when you hear greater works stories, you find you want to experience your own.

As I walked through the store with my family, I began praying in my heart, "Lord, I want to be bolder, more courageous. Father, give me cool stories. Let me see the way You see as I walk through my day." One of the salesladies walked by and suddenly my Father whispered to my heart, "Ask her if you can pray for her sick husband." I hadn't expected Him to give me such a specific story so quickly and in such a public place.

I am a fairly reserved person, both in taste and personality. I tend to wear grey, or slate, or granite…and sometimes steel blue. I sit in the back, unless I have to sit in the front. I keep to myself. I don't get real animated. I have only danced in public three times. Once on my first date with Karen—I felt it a necessary sacrifice to get the girl. The two other occasions were at weddings.

I imagine I look like Gene Kelly when I dance—easy, confident, and classy, like jazz. But I probably look more like Carlton. Many who witnessed us Clarks on the dance floor at my sister's wedding (the second time I danced) thought we might have had too much to drink. But there was no alcohol at her wedding. And at my brother Joel's wedding (which was the third time), it was the kids who suckered me into moving in ways I'm not designed.

You know King David, one of my favorite Old Testament characters. He once worshiped God by dancing in front of a nation in his underwear (see 2 Sam. 6:13-15). He looked foolish. He looked crazy. But there are times when foolish and crazy are the correct postures. Honestly, on this untamed journey, I am learning that sometimes worship can look foolish and crazy. But I want to live my life in response to His presence; I want the story. So I am learning to say yes, even when it's caused discomfort.

I headed toward the saleswoman, I was a little nervous, but at least I wasn't dancing, and I was completely clothed. Before I could reach her, she went into the back. EMPLOYEES ONLY the sign read. I wasn't sure what I was supposed to do next. I wasn't even positive I'd heard God right, but I really didn't want to miss a chance for a good story.

Me: "Father, tell Ya what, if she comes back out with something in her left hand, spins twice, and her right shoe is untied, I will go speak to her."

God: "How about you just speak to her when she comes back out?"

Me: "Yes."

She did, and I did. "Excuse me," I said, "but are you married?"

"Yes," she said, confused.

"Is your husband sick?"

"Yes." Now *she* looked uncomfortable.

I smiled, not because I was happy her husband was sick, but I *was* happy. "God loves you both so much that He told me about your husband and I believe He wants me to pray for Him," I said in a rush.

Her eyes welled up with tears and she told me her story. Her husband had recently gone to Chicago on a business trip and had become ill. He spent seven days in his hotel room until finally a friend had flown up to help take him to a hospital where he had spent the last few days.

Right in the store, we took a moment. I prayed for her husband. Then we traded e-mail addresses. Later I received an e-mail that her husband was home and well. Crazy? Yes. A cool story? Absolutely. I think the best stories are the ones where risk is involved, where we have to step past comfortable. I think the best stories, the ones filled with promise, are the ones that feel a little scary. I want the best stories.

Scary Is Fun

I want to live this life in the brilliance of Your song
I want to worship You with a life fully sung...a beautiful song

We were on vacation in the wild Northwest—Vancouver Island, to be specific. My daughter Maddy was almost three years old. I was treading water at the deep end of the local public indoor pool. She was on the diving board. It was at least as far away from the water as she was tall, and she was tall for her age. It had been her idea to jump and had seemed like a good idea from the shallow end. I waited below the diving board, encouraging her, but to no avail. It was "too high" and "too scary."

Earlier in the week, I had gone cliff jumping, a good seventy feet of it. I love rivers and have an unwavering opinion they have been created for my enjoyment. So when I see a river, I generally want to get in it. How I get in it is where the fun begins.

Pete, a good friend from the area, and I had hiked out to the river and spent about an hour swimming at the bottom of its beautiful seventy-foot waterfall. After we finished swimming, we began the climb back up the trail. The trail switched back and forth up the side of the falls, and we arrived at the top just in time to watch dumbfounded as some fella jumped into the water below.

Both Pete and I have done some cliff jumping in our day, but when we first saw the falls, we hadn't even considered it—it was really high. But once I saw the guy's head pop out of the water, I realized it could be done without dying. And so while Pete, with his back to me, talked to one of the jumper's friends at the cliff edge, I talked to myself.

"It's just two steps and you're over the edge." My eyes focused on the edge. "Just two steps," I whispered to myself as I took a deep breath. "Just two steps." I removed my shoes. "Just two steps," I whispered as I took off my shirt. "Just two steps." I took another breath and then took the two steps, and as I dropped, I sensed Pete turn and I heard him say, "Oh, Jason!"

It was an amazing experience and also a great story. One Pete and I have told and relived in the telling many times since. You see,

Pete is not one to watch someone else get a good story without him. Within ten seconds, he had followed me over the edge. I still smile when picturing him eye rolling and muttering under his breath while quickly removing his shoes and shirt and then taking those two steps.

When we got back to the hotel, Maddy heard our stories. Now it's hard to explain to a three-year-old why anyone would jump off a cliff. Three-year-olds don't have the capacity to understand this. The best I could do by way of explanation is say, "Sometimes scary is fun."

So as I treaded water under the diving board, I reminded her again. "Honey, sometimes scary is fun!" She was a hard sell, but I persisted until we finally came to an agreement—I would jump with her. I joined her on the diving board. "It's just two steps."

I would love to tell you it wasn't too high, her head didn't go under, and there was nothing but joy in her eyes. But that would be a lie. The truth is that Maddy kept a death grip on me until we reached the side of the pool; she was convinced she had made a mistake. But once we were safe, she began to laugh at the wonder of it all. I did too.

My little girl beat the diving board. Yes, it was too scary and too high, but she did it anyway. She jumped—for herself, for me, for the story. Years later, most of that vacation has faded from her memory, but the story of the diving board lives on. And "scary is fun" has become a household phrase.

Let me give you a father's perspective. Before and after she jumped, I was enthusiastic in my encouragement. When we reached the side of the pool, I was immersed in her joy. For the rest of the week, I was overwhelmed with pride. She had believed; she had lived fully untamed and I got to be a part of it. I was her catalyst, her savior, and her friend. And together we beat the diving board. The wonder of my daughter's trust and then the opportunity to be faithful with it are a father's dream come true. If she had not jumped, we both would have missed out. But she did jump and now she owns the story. She owns that experience. And the diving board no longer controls her fear.

It's a great story.

The Safest and Most Dangerous Story

God is not trying to keep you safe.
He is trying to keep you from a meaningless life![1]

Years ago I led worship in a church that we had just started attending. As I was finishing the last song, I invited everyone in the room to say yes to whatever God was asking. It was a simple invitation to trust Him, even if it was uncomfortable. It was also an invitation to experience Him and discover our story. I was gentle but insistent. I waited a few minutes before praying over everyone. It was sweet and sincere. There were some tears as people discovered His love. There was joy and hope, which are all good signs we have met with God. As a worshiper, there is nothing like leading people who have positioned their hearts with a yes.

Afterward, the very friendly pastor thanked me. "That was amazing. I loved it!" he said. Then he continued with a phrase Karen and me now use when we think something is crazy: "You are two weeks and a tambourine ahead of us." I was never asked to lead worship by that pastor again. I now understand he was both complimenting me and graciously dismissing me. I also understand why. My worship wasn't safe, at least not in a way that was comfortable.

Safe. It's a wonderful word. It means, "to be free from hurt, injury, danger, or risk." It's funny how we can use that word to correctly define God's love and yet we all know we can't use that word to define a life of following God. It's almost as if that word, when it comes to God, is a paradox.

Comfortable is another of these words. Comforter is one of the names for the Holy Spirit and yet there is nothing comfortable in being led by Him. Jesus lived in this paradox. He knew His Father in such a way that He was secure, sure, safe. He walked daily with the Comforter and yet lived a most uncomfortable and risky life—even unto death. While He was the safest person on the planet, He was also the most dangerous.

The invitation I gave that Sunday morning in worship was one of discovering the Safest Person on the planet and in so doing discover our own *scary is fun* untamed story.

Pastors are shepherds by nature; they have a primary and beautiful focus, which is to protect the sheep. I have heard the message time and again, from the pulpit, over coffee, or in a church lobby: "We want to provide a safe place for people to come and worship." Yes, but a safe place should never be synonymous with a domesticated people.

There must be opportunities in a safe environment to risk, to step out, to be uncomfortably obedient, to lay down our lives, to surrender, to worship with passion, to discover the wonder of His presence—revelation must be the primary focus.

I think much of our current church culture has confused a safe place with a tamed people. We are not to be tamed and domesticated; we are created to be passionate and powerfully free. We are designed to live in the same paradox Jesus revealed. Our churches should be the safest places on the planet while empowering sons and daughters to live dangerously untamed with all of heaven at our back.

I have given my life to the revolutionary who goes by the name *Jesus* and there has been nothing safe in following Him. I have invited the Comforter to take the lead and there has been nothing comfortable about it.

If we allow comfort and safety to define our worship, we step away from intimacy and into religious form. I once saw a bumper sticker that illustrates this well: "Take your kids to Sunday school this Sunday, they need and deserve it." The problem with this statement is my kids don't need Sunday school; they need an encounter with Father, Son, and Holy Spirit. We may learn about Him in Sunday school, but the sticker's premise is completely wrong. If you want to lose a generation, raise them to know the names of God but never experience the interpretations—Loving, Intimate, Majestic, Holy, Consuming Fire.

We were born for communion with God. Our hearts are designed for wild worship, yet we're often offered rote liturgy. Our minds are designed to dream as big as the heart of God, but we're immersed in the latest building plans. Our bodies are designed for dangerous service; we're taught biblical commentaries from the safety of a pew or a comfortable theater chair.

Please understand, I'm not challenging how we structure a Sunday morning service, I'm challenging why we gather together in the first place. There is nothing wrong with liturgy—the Bible is filled with it. There's nothing wrong with building plans—I like to worship under a roof, especially when it's cold, hot or raining outside. And Scripture is beautiful and essential—it's an invitation to personally know Him. But at the end of the day, if we haven't *experienced* revelation, if we haven't *experienced* His goodness, if we haven't encountered His nature—evidence of one of His many names—then the gathering is nothing more than a Christian social club. I'm all for Sunday school if it drives us headlong into Jesus and our story. He must be experienced.

God has invited us into our very own faith stories. They are the stories entered into through discomfort, the ones full of "too high" and "too scary." But we jump anyway because living in response to the Holy Spirit makes for the safest yet most dangerous stories. And they're really the only ones worth living.

Six Floors and an Escort

I will stay awhile, let my heart beat with Yours,
I'm dancing to Your melody
And I can feel You, see You, know You, praise You,
You're everything to me

Aimee is my sister. She has always felt deeply; she loves big. Everything about her is authentic. She doesn't put on airs, and when she gives you a compliment, which she often does, it releases such life because there is no falseness in it.

My sister loves Joel's motto—do it for the story. She has been saying yes to God's uncomfortable and yet beautiful invitations to discover her own story for a long time. Years ago Aimee was driving by a hospital near her home when she felt God tugging on her heart: "Go in there and love the people."

Aimee believes God is a healer. Her passion is to see people walking whole and free and loved. When someone needs prayer, she is a bold champion. But walking alone into a hospital to pray for people felt scary and maybe even a little foolish. The idea made her terribly uncomfortable.

As she walked into the hospital, she asked God to lead her to someone who really needed a visit. There were six floors in the hospital, so, with nothing other than God's invitation, she decided she'd start on the first and work her way up to the sixth floor.

First Floor

Now there are rules about this sort of thing. You can't just go walking through a hospital. Aimee wasn't interested in breaking rules; she was there to love and honor everyone, including the nurses. So she made her way to the first-floor desk. There was a wall of glass between her and the nurse. Aimee, uncomfortable because she had never done this before, leaned in and asked the nurse if there was anyone who might be in need of a visit. "Maybe someone who doesn't have family around," she said.

The first-floor nurse immediately teared up. Then she got really close to the glass and spoke softly, "There is a girl on this floor who really needs prayer. I can't tell you who it is or her room number, but she is in isolation." Aimee, pleasantly surprised by the welcome, simply said, "Thanks," and went in search of the girl in isolation. She wasn't able to go in so she prayed in the hallway and then headed for the second floor.

The nurse met her at the elevator: "Thank you for being here! Keep listening to that still small voice." Then she hugged Aimee tightly.

Second Floor

Aimee couldn't find a nurse so she just walked down a hall. On her left, in a hospital bed, lay a woman watching *The Price Is Right*. She walked in, introduced herself. The lady's name was Faye.

"Faye, I was driving by the hospital and felt like I was supposed to stop by and visit you," Aimee said. "Is there anything I can pray for?" Faye told her story—she was anemic and had passed out in Wal-Mart. She woke up at the hospital. Aimee asked if she could pray for Faye's condition. "I don't ever refuse prayer," Faye said. "Me neither," Aimee replied. She loved on Faye, just like Jesus.

Third Floor

On the third floor, Aimee found a nurse at the station. She was getting better at this, and with a little more confidence she again asked if there was anyone she could visit with. This third-floor nurse didn't tear up. She only looked at Aimee suspiciously, and said, "Everyone on the third floor is just fine." Aimee, uncomfortable again, quietly thanked her and headed for the fourth floor.

Fourth Floor

Another nurses' station, another nurse. More tears. "Really? You came here to visit someone? That's amazing. I have to find someone for you, surely there is someone. Come with me. This is so sweet, you came to visit someone, so sweet...." The nurse hardly took a breath.

In the end, they couldn't find anyone. "I can't believe someone finally came and we have no one. I'm so sorry," the nurse said through tears. She hugged Aimee like she was family and Aimee hugged her, just like Jesus.

Fifth Floor

She stepped off the elevator and was met by the fifth-floor nurse who was waiting for her. More tears and hugs. She pointed her to the room of an eighty-seven-year-old woman. Her name was Margaret and she wasn't well. She was so small in the bed—fragile. Confused when she met Aimee, but she warmed quickly when Aimee told her she had come to hear her story.

"Sit down, dear," she said as she motioned to a chair. Margaret was hard of hearing and even harder to understand. She spoke softly. She had four children, her husband was still alive, they lived in Franklin, Tennessee her whole life, and she was at the hospital because she almost had a heart attack.

Aimee talked about her family, her two girls, and her husband, Eric. Then she prayed quietly for Margaret and Margaret's living husband and kids. Just before leaving, Aimee brushed Margaret's silver hair back off her face and told her she had the most beautiful eyes.

Aimee left Margaret in prayer. "Father, I want to love more, I want to have my own stories of Your love. I want to see Your miracles released through me. I want to practice giving freely what You have so generously given me." Aimee was there for love, for the story.

Sixth Floor

This time it was a tall security guard who greeted her as she exited the elevator. He asked kindly, "Why are you here, miss?"

"I'm visiting people."

"Whom are you visiting?" he asked.

"Anyone the nurses tell me I can—those who don't get many visitors."

Before Aimee had finished talking, another guard showed up. One guard was a little daunting, two guards, well.... "Is there a 'visiting hospital patients jail'?" she wondered. This guy was shorter and less kind. He started asking the same questions with one addition: "Who were you looking for on the third floor?" Apparently the third-floor nurse had called in the cavalry.

He took her ID and went to a phone. She was left with the first guard who was writing notes down in a little pad. Aimee noticed the sixth-floor nurses were glaring at her like she was a criminal. They held her until the chairman of the hospital showed up in a huff, white coat and all. "We have people for this, miss," he scolded.

"I understand," Aimee said. She was well past comfortable and feeling foolish.

"Show her out," he said to the tall guard.

Walking to the elevator like a little girl being accompanied by her teacher to see the principal, Aimee said, "I don't need to be escorted. I'll go."

"It's just policy, ma'am," the kind guard said.

Once the elevator doors closed, he touched Aimee's arm. "Hold your head up! You heard that still small voice and you responded.

Don't let this discourage you. You have no idea the impact your obedience had on this hospital."

On the elevator ride down, he continued to encourage her. As he walked Aimee to her car, he said something that seemed to contradict everything that was happening. "Aimee, you are welcome anytime." It's a funny thing to say to someone you are escorting off the premises, but that was what he said. He recognized the truth amidst opposition. Aimee was there on God's authority.

I love this story, not because there was some grand earth shattering miracle at the end but because of her grand earth shattering *yes* to His invitation to trust Him and in so doing discover more of her story. I love Aimee's willingness to continue from one floor to the next, to continue to say yes even when uncomfortable, even when she wasn't sure what she was doing, when it felt foolish and looked crazy.

Aimee didn't get some wild miracle but the miracle wasn't the point, her trust was the point. While there wasn't some clear and obvious breakthrough, let me be clear, there was powerful breakthrough in and for Aimee. You see, when the Father says, "Hey, Aimee, let's go to a hospital and pray for people," He knows she will say yes. He knows she can be trusted with greater revelation and understanding. He knows the yes today leads to the greater works promise tomorrow. Her willingness to act crazy and feel foolish for the sake of the story, for the sake of love, will lead her into greater and more powerful stories.

Aimee is my hero. She loves well and she has many stories of God's love and power in her life—stories where she took the two steps and jumped. She is willing to be uncomfortable and a little scared. She is willing to appear foolish and crazy. And she is also willing to break some rules. And while I understand rules have a purpose, the hospital story wasn't really about the rules; it was about trust and risk. It was about Aimee doing it for her story.

Break Some Rules

So rise up, oh bride of God
Be faithful with your trust

At the beginning of this chapter I noted how I come from a family of storytellers. Well, you could also say it this way: I come from a family of rule breakers. You see, the best stories are always the ones that break some rules.

My family, we are not much into rules, especially the religious rules that box us in and conform us to an apathetic, uninspired, domesticated existence. You know, the stupid rules, the rules that restrain us to living a "safe" expression of Christianity and remove us from the miraculous birthright we are meant to experience, the rules that limit God and therefore make for a boring story.

My family collects religious rule-breaking stories like Chuck Norris collects Chuck Norris quotes. Sometimes the religious rules have to be broken. For instance...

- Sometimes I don't go to church on Sunday morning. Instead, I sleep in and then make a big breakfast with my family. We call it pancake church.

- Sometimes I tip more than 15 percent.

- Sometimes I see "sinners" the way my Father sees them—I'm believing for an "always" in this category.

- Sometimes I pray *after* I eat and I keep my eyes open while doing it.

- Sometimes I smoke Cubans with my brothers and I really enjoy it.

- Sometimes I stop people in stores or on the street and pray for them.

- Sometimes I enjoy music on Christian radio, but most of the time I prefer the independent music scene.

- Sometimes I worship with abandon and it makes the comfortable angry.

- Sometimes I give money to the fella on the street corner even though it's possible he will buy alcohol with it. His possible actions don't get to determine my actual generosity.

- Sometimes I slide our tithe under my neighbor's door instead of putting it in the basket that's passed around on Sunday.

- Sometimes I use mild cuss words to tell a story that my editor has to later remove.

- Sometimes I'm late on my mortgage, while at other times I make a lot of money. Either way, I don't feel guilty about it.

- Sometimes when I live in the confidence of a saint, I ruffle the feathers of those convinced we are all hopeless sinners.

- Sometimes I tell miracle stories and make those who don't believe in miracles uncomfortable.

The list goes on and on, but you get it. Some rules are made to be broken, like the socially uncomfortable interaction with a store clerk, or the rule-breaking trust of my sister, Aimee. My point is simply that our heavenly Father loves a good story, the one where we discover who He is and how we are made. The one where we seek the experience with Him and with His people, where we are willing to break away from the bureaucracy of religious rules to know the best story.

The Best Story

It is abnormal for a Christian not to have an appetite for the impossible. It has been written into our spiritual DNA to hunger for the impossibilities around us to bow at the name of Jesus.

I believe the best stories are the ones God is telling. They are always about family, because family *is* the story. His stories revolve around Love like the earth revolves around the sun, and they are always about a future and a hope.

My greatest prayer is that I live an inspired story, the best story, a story my kids will tell their kids one day. And that's really the point, that we would live stories that inspire, empower, and create a future and hope in those around us and for those who follow after.

Have you ever wondered why when we were kids the Bible stories read to us were meant to inspire dreams of impossibilities being made possible with God? And yet as adults, the same stories become observations of how it was "once upon a time." Why is it the radical miracle stories of my youth found in the Bible have become tamed three-point sermons I could comfortably and safely apply to my life now that I am an adult?

When I was a child it was possible for boys to kill evil giants and men to walk on water. When I was a child it was possible to live inside a whale, a raging fire, and a lion's den. When I was a child it was possible to pray for the sick and watch them recover. Shadows could heal and the dead could be raised. When I was a child I believed with God all impossibilities were possible.

The best stories are the ones where life's impossibilities—failures, pains, betrayals, disillusionments, fears, deaths—become possibilities. If you are reading this and you no longer believe as a child, but everything in you wants to, try this statement on for size: "Father, I want to believe with You that all impossibilities are possible. Show me how."

Now here's the thing (and I should have warned you of this first), after you pray this you will begin to hear our Father's invitation to step into your own uncomfortable, risky, seemingly foolish, rule-breaking story. But it will be good, because all of His stories are full of the wonder of His miraculous love. Sounds a little scary? Sounds a little fun? That's the whole point. Remember, sometimes scary is fun.

Be Strong and Jump

So give me the land of giants, give me the other side
For I am Your believer and we won't be denied

Okay, here's my message. I'm not on a soapbox, but down on a kneeler, all right? Humbly bowed before the Author of the story. Be strong and courageous. There is great risk involved in following Jesus, yet the only way to live the promise, to live life to its fullest, is found in the passionate pursuit of the Author of life. It's not safe, rarely easy, and never boring. It's often hard, scary, and death defying. It's a miracle upon miracle, life-giving adventure.

God *is* safe. But it's a safety found in relationship, a safety that can be experienced in the discomfort of radical obedience, in profound trust, in reckless conformity to the heart of our Father. My safety and your safety is discovered in a relationship where we say yes to God, yes to trusting, yes to obeying, and yes to believing, and then taking those two steps and jumping.

God is raising revolutionaries—men and women who will walk surrendered and untamed lives of worship, willing adventurers living wholly for His glory, risking all to walk beside their Savior. God is growing up generations who will accept nothing less than a real experience with Him. They want to stand before burning bushes, they want to wrestle with angels, they want to run for the Promised

Land and expand its borders. The cross is beautiful to them, the resurrection stunning.

We have discovered that "scary is fun," we have a yes written on our hearts, and we are doing it for the story…because God loves a good story.

I want to fight, I want to weep, I want to give,
I want to reap, I want to live and believe

Endnote

1.   Kris Vallotton, *Purity* (Shippensburg, PA: Destiny Image, 2008).

2.   Bill Johnson, *Face to Face with God* (Lake Mary, FL: Charisma House, 2007).

Chapter 6

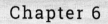

Giant Killers

Rock Throwing

There's a cry in my spirit
So loud you can hear it
My soul's awakening

"I'm going to kill you!" he screamed.

"God, help me! Save me!" I prayed.

Wait. Let me back up just a bit. You need a little context for this drama. I was ten years old, which in my opinion was much too young to die. We had clearly underestimated this guy's speed. He was fast, like "run the forty in 4.5 seconds" fast, and he was mad. I was fast too, but not that fast.

My friend Chris had asked if I thought he could actually skip the stone across the water and hit the neighborhood bully on the other side.

"No way!" I said. "But I'd like to see you try."

"Okay," he said with a wicked smile. Then, not being complete idiots, we discussed the situation and worst-case scenario in case Chris pulled off this miracle.

First, let me describe the situation. The kid across the water was a bully. We had once witnessed him knee another boy in the face. In terms of neighborhood justice, this kid had it coming, whatever "it" was. Second, if the worst-case scenario occurred, Chris's house wasn't that far away—only about a hundred-yard run through the park and then six houses down. A river separated the bully from us, and the only bridge in the park was at least thirty yards in the wrong direction. All we'd really have to do is run like mad and we would be safe.

And then it happened. Chris crossed over into the legends of rock skippers. In one singular motion, he twisted slightly, cocked his arm, stepped forward, snapped his wrist, and released pure vengeance into the air. It was the throw of a lifetime—the trajectory and spin were such that it was obvious—this throw was the will of God. Time slowed, almost to a stop, and we witnessed the rock dance across the river's surface, finally thumping squarely in the bully's stomach. I kid you not.

All right, I'll cut to the chase, so to speak. Our satisfaction was short-lived, all of about a nanosecond as the bully sought and then discovered the source of his affliction. His face turned from surprise to rage, and terror gripped us both. "Run!" we screamed.

As I ran, I remembered the preacher's joke from a few weeks earlier, about how when you run from a bear, it's not important that you're fast, just that you're faster than the guy next to you. Chris must have heard the same joke because he kicked it into warp five.

There are moments, even when you're ten years old, that you realize "I'm not going to make it out of this alive." I had such a moment. I made a decision based purely on survival instinct. Instead of running down the sidewalk, I dove into a hedge and assumed the fetal position. I lay perfectly still, attempting the old Jedi mind trick: "Nothing to see here, be on your way." But I was not yet a Jedi.

The bully suddenly jumped through the hedge and he was carrying the largest rock I'd ever seen. I don't know where or when he found it, but he had it cocked over his head and I knew this was the end.

"I'm going to kill you!" he screamed.

"God, help me! Save me!" I prayed. And then God answered my prayer in a woman's voice—a terrifyingly beautiful voice. Chris had made it safely home, alerting his mom to the crisis, and she was running up the sidewalk, yelling, putting the fear of God in the bully, while cementing the existence of God in me. The bully dropped the rock and ran for his life. Signs and wonders, people...signs and wonders.

I have several stories like this from my childhood, oddly most of them involving Chris. As with most boy stories, the facts got a little skewed along the way to accentuate our heroic status. Eventually even the bully-in-the-park debacle was transformed into a tale of epic conquest; Chris's mom didn't even make an appearance. But in all fairness, last time I checked, David's mom wasn't there when he killed Goliath.

Why am I telling you this story? Because life is full of giants. They are found in business, education, and family. They can look like financial hardship, sickness, or an obstacle hampering advancement at a job. Giants are the things in our life that seek to cause fear through intimidation or worry through uncertainty; they are the seemingly overwhelming circumstances that stand between our promise and us. In order to move forward in life, in order to discover the fullness of our promise, we have to defeat them.

I believe each giant in life represents a promise, and typically, the bigger the giant the bigger the promise. But the moment God gives us the promise is the moment the giant's fate is sealed. *For from Him and through Him and to Him are all things* (Rom. 11:36). God holds the beginning and the end, and through Him the giant doesn't have a chance. We were born to kill giants.

But instead of letting God choose my giants, I've often picked them myself. I've assumed I knew best how to define my promise. Using my brilliant and ambitious mind as a compass, making calculations, and basing my decisions on the fact the giant is indeed bad, I would then analyze the risk, throw my rock, and, well, you know how that ends. All too many times, after exhaustion and tears, I've found myself huddled in the fetal position, crying out, "God, save me! Help me! I don't want to die." Thankfully God has shown up with His beautifully terrifying voice just in time.

But when God is my compass, when His love and peace are my daily companions, the scenario changes. When I attack a giant, it's not some random "good idea," it's the specific giant that stands between God's promise and myself. I am not just trying my luck, I am operating in the authority He gave when He established the promise in my heart. The question changes from, what might happen if I do? to, what will I miss if I don't? I'm not throwing a rock and running away. I'm running straight ahead with heart, soul, mind, and strength. The question is no longer, will this work? but, what is the revelation and where will it lead me? It's about what kind of believing I can possess and what impact my believing will have in advancing the Kingdom.

A Violent Believer

No risk without danger. No faith if I'm sure,
I'm not but I'm absolutely positive in the way I'll live
Surrendered and untamed, whole and insane

His name is Harnish—Shawn Harnish. He's been a part of my life since the early Fringe days. He does everything, and most of it all at once. He could dismantle an atomic bomb while preparing pan-roasted duck breast, steamed root vegetables, and speckled butter beans for a party of ten, while playing Mancala—the 7,000-year-old Arabic board game—with his daughter. I don't believe Shawn has ever done any of these things, but he could if he wanted too.

I used to think hockey was God's favorite sport, but over the course of a few years Harnish convinced me God's game is indeed football—the NFL. And after taking me to a Buffalo Bills game, he convinced me they were God's favorite team. He also convinced his boys of that when they were very young. Now they're old enough for Harnish to relive his glory days through them.

Harnish lives in western New York. Our phone conversations are usually long; we talk about God, church, family, but at some point we always talk about football. We talked just the other day. His boys had started football season, and he'd told them, "Football is a game of wild abandon, and you can't play scared. You'll never be an impact player if you do."

He went on to tell me his oldest, Tyler, took quite a hit the other day, and for a moment Harnish wondered how he would play on the next possession. Tyler shook the hit off and remembered the other piece of instruction his dad had given him: "It is better to give than to receive." I love the fact that Harnish is teaching his boys the Bible. I also love the fact he just assumes his boys want to be impact players.

I believe God just assumes we want to be impact players too. None of us were called to be benchwarmers; there is no such thing as a mediocre promise in the Kingdom of God. But let's not kid ourselves, we are playing a violent game—life is not all daisies and snow cones. Jesus told us, *The kingdom of heaven suffers violence, and violent men take it by force*" (Matt. 11:12 NKJV). There are evils in this world: sickness, hunger, poverty, abuse, hate. But there are also violent believers who are sure in His love.

A violent believer is intimate with the heart of God, knows surrender in its purest form—in other words, trust—and has the courage to risk. He or she sees the giant and says, "You're mine," and then runs at it with a sling.

Embracing our promise will always start with surrender to God. In that surrender we experience and possess the truths we will need to advance and the authority to run at life with wild abandon. Surrender to God is the most violent thing a person can do with their life because it is directly connected to the destruction of evil. Violence is an act of faith that sets captives free, releases joy to those in sorrow, empowers the weak, heals the sick and feeds the hungry. When we live as violent believers, the miraculous always follows. Sorta like this next story.

The McDonald's Miracle

I want to see as You see
I want to dream what You dream
To be what You made me

Years ago my brother Joel was living in South Africa working as a youth pastor. He was headed back to his apartment one day after having been up early and serving a mission team late into the night. Exhausted and hungry, he drove past a McDonald's. The idea of a hamburger, fries, and a Coke seemed the perfect way to unwind at the end of this day. As he walked in, a few homeless street kids stood around the entrance. This wasn't unusual, but as he started to order his Biggie-Size Mac Meal, something else was—he heard God whisper, "Buy the boys some hamburgers."

Joel was tired and only had enough rand (South African currency) for his meal. He was slightly annoyed, thinking, "I've worked all day and I don't even have enough money to get myself everything I want, let alone feed the kids outside." But because Joel was *learning* how to live violently believing, he ran headlong into what he believed God was asking him to do.

He bought as many burgers as he could afford, five total. But as he walked out of the restaurant, he saw there were seven kids. He didn't have enough, plus the chances of him getting one were slim. But if you have the authority to run at a giant, it's foolish to turn back. He began passing out burgers to the boys outside.

Now this really gets good. As Joel passed out burgers, more kids from across the street saw what he was doing and began to make their way toward him. Still, he just kept obeying what God had said to him, following through on the invitation—he kept saying yes. And somewhere between God's whisper and way too many mouths to feed, it dawned on him that he should have run out of burgers long ago. But he didn't.

Suddenly Joel wasn't tired anymore. Suddenly Joel was having fun. When he handed the last boy a burger, he looked in the bag. Yeah, you guessed it—one left over, just for Joel.

I Believe, Help My Unbelief

Jesus asked the boy's father, "How long has he been like this?" "From childhood," he answered. "It has often thrown him into fire or water to kill him. But if You can do anything, take pity on us and help us." "'If You can'?" said Jesus. "Everything is possible for him who believes." Immediately the boy's father exclaimed, "I do believe; help me overcome my unbelief!" (Mark 9:21-24)

Apparently the disciples had prayed over this boy who was possessed by an evil spirit, but their prayers had no effect on him. The boy remained tormented. The crowd waited to see how Jesus would handle the situation. He questioned the boy's father about his condition and got a "please, if you can do anything" response.

If Jesus could do anything?

What amazes me is even though I have a direct line to the God who created the universe, I still find myself saying "if." What's more amazing is that my Father knows this and so He provides me with opportunities to step out and experience the miraculous even when I'm not feeling it. Case in point is Joel's multiplying hamburger miracle. With his actions, my brother chose to believe, and because he did, the miraculous broke in. This may not appear violent on the surface, but it is—anytime the miraculous takes place, a "giant" dies, and anytime a bell rings, an angel gets his wings….

The "violent take it by force" believing lifestyle isn't about blood and guts, it's about trusting in God's love and then stepping out regardless of the risk. It's about living in a way where we constantly cry, "I believe, help my unbelief." Regardless of our physical, emotional, or mental state, God is always inviting us to surrender and step out beyond our comfort zone into physically, emotionally, and intellectually challenging scenarios so He can uniquely meet us, reveal His love, and empower us into our promise. This radical and violent believing always advances His Kingdom.

Oh, and by the way, Jesus healed and set that boy free.

Living Later Now

Faith dwells on the edge of presumption[1]

When God gives us a promise, the only way to own it is to live like we believe He's good for it. It's called living later now—at least, I think that's a cool way to describe it. We must learn to live actively waiting, prepared for any God moment.

I mentioned that one of my favorite childhood Bible stories involved the boy born to be king—David. Think about him. After he heard the promise from Samuel, David went back to herding sheep; however, something major had shifted in his heart. He began to adjust his thinking from "I am a shepherd" to "I will be a king." This is profound as it means he began engaging his promise immediately. And because he did this, when Goliath presented himself, David saw it as an attack on "his kingdom" and acted as a king should. David whirled his sling, released the rock, and killed the giant. This was David's giant, the one who stood smack in front of his promise.

It's about living later now. David heard his promise and then went back up into the hills to herd sheep. But I think he went back up there believing and therefore living the promise even before Goliath presented himself. This kind of believing empowered David to pull who he was going to be—a king—into his present circumstances. And when the opportunity came to act, he was ready. He killed a giant.

The same goes for you and me. We may hear our promise and then go back to teaching school or changing oil or whatever it is we do, but if we can begin to believe, by our words and actions, that the promise is true, then we begin to engage our promise. Then when the giant shows his face, we won't be devising exit strategies or escape routes. Instead, we will violently believe.

Our promises are not guaranteed. They are more like a glimpse of how we have been designed and who we can become if we believe, surrender, and live with wild abandon. It's when our believing is aligned with God's promise that we possess the authority to kill giants. When the opportunity comes knocking, we can answer it bravely.

Wilde with an "E"

There's a violent hunger in my bones
'Cause I've tasted and I've seen
There's a lion roaring in my heart
And I've determined to set Him free

My son's middle name is Wilde—Ethan Wilde, with an "e." Karen and I had been discussing middle names for months, and one night while lying in bed, she said, "What about Wild?" There was about a thirty-second pause before I said with much sincerity, "I wish my middle name was Wild!" So it was decided then and there that "Wild" would be his middle name. We had no idea what kind of reaction this was going to cause with our mothers.

"You don't want to name him that!" they assured us.

"What if he turns out wild or violent?" they asked.

That was the whole point, but we added an "e" to the end of Wild thinking that might help the grandmothers, plus it's English and sophisticated. But in no way do we expect the addition of an "e" to civilize or tame the meaning of the word.

My son is kind and gentle and wild and he is one of the coming revolutionaries in the church. He is growing into a man that will help God's people redefine the word *wild*, to reveal the absolute essential nature of violently advancing God's Kingdom. It has nothing to do with being unkind or out of control and everything to do with knowing and living abandoned in the pleasure of the King. It's about daring to live each and every day in a posture of worship, owning our Father's dreams as our own and pursuing them as if our very lives depended on it. Because they do. They really do.

Divine Insanity

Surrendered and untamed
Whole and insane

By the way, did you know God is insane? He searches throughout the world for fellow lunatics. He is always recruiting. His one prerequisite is absolute surrender to His uncomfortable, unreasonable, illogical, impossible, and sometimes life-threatening will. He wants violent, believing lunatics. I know it doesn't say that literally in the Bible, but it's there. Trust me.

Look at any hero of the faith and you'll see they all had moments of divine insanity. Noah to Abraham, Gideon to Peter, Martin Luther to Mother Teresa—they each had moments where they believed, stepped into the promises from God, acted like utter fools, stood toe to toe with their giants, and history was never the same.

There is nothing safe in believing; there are no guarantees that we will come through with all our body parts intact or that a bully won't heft a rock and threaten to kill us or that a deceiver won't promise us the wealth of the world if we'll just bend the knee and worship him. There's also no guarantee we won't literally die trying.

> "Well, you may not know this, but there's things that gnaw at a man worse than dying."
>
> —CHARLEY WAITE, Open Range

There are things worse than dying, like always wondering what might have been if we'd just trusted and acted or spoken or loved. A life filled with regret has nothing to do with the Kingdom. We're either running toward, or running away. I'm sorry, but there's no third choice.

Surrendering empowers me to live as an untamed, violently believing, God-loving lunatic who is pushing further and further into his promises each day. It's the most violent thing I can do. Some days it's big and obvious, like burgers multiplying by the handful. Other days it's gentle and quiet, like a renewed sense of love for my wife, my daughters, and my son, and a commitment to keep on running headlong into the plans my Father has for me. Whatever it is, it's always miraculous. It really is.

Endnote

1.   Graham Cooke, *When Heaven Opens* (Salt Lake City: Aardvark Global Publishing, 2007).

Chapter 7

Relevant

A Goodly Sum

I believe the stars are falling, every one a seed of fire
And I believe a wave is coming to birth a holy pure desire

We were walking the densely crowded halls of a conference for The Church Leaders of Tomorrow—at least that's what the pamphlet indicated. We were "rubbing elbows" with attendees and checking out the conference booths that circled the arena. I was feeling distracted and slightly annoyed, and trying to figure out why. I had a Switchfoot song running through my head—"I don't belong here, feels like I don't belong."[1] Then I realized Jeremy, one of my closest friends, had introduced me to another pastor. This nice fella was talking to me. So I focused back in: "...we have almost two hundred members now!" he said, and he was looking right at me.

"I can swim from one end of the pool to the other in one breath," I thought but thankfully didn't say. "Feels like I don't belong...." The song was still running through my head and Reverend Nice was still looking at me. Quickly, searching my mind, I latched onto the last thing he said. "Two hundred members! Really? Wow! That's a goodly sum!"

A goodly sum? Really?

Minutes later we were walking away from yet another conversation about how relevant a church was due to its growth in attendance. All we had talked about were numbers—how many on a Sunday morning, a Wednesday night—it wouldn't be long and they'd need their own building. I think he was married, but that's due to my stellar powers of observation and the wedding ring on his finger. Once again I'd celebrated a pastor's sincere definition of success. And once again I found myself frustrated in doing so.

I love to celebrate success. There is nothing better than rejoicing with people in their breakthrough. I absolutely believe in church growth, but here's the rub: I don't believe church attendance numbers are the true indicator of a successful church, and they certainly don't determine relevancy.

"Are you as frustrated as I am?" I asked Jeremy.

"What do you mean?"

"Well, either I'm missing something or I'm the most irrelevant person here."

"Why?" Jeremy asked.

"Because my current church only has four members. One of them is married to me and the other three are pretty wide-eyed. If I tell them there is a lion in the backyard, and if we want to see it we have to quietly sneak out the front door and crawl along the side of the house so as not to spook it—they're right behind me. Or if I tell them that we Clarks have a special tiny hole at the tip of our thumbs, too small to see, but if you put the thumb in your mouth just right and blow hard enough, it will make your leg kick out. Well, again, they believe me. So they may not count. Bottom line, my church may not be relevant."

I continued. "So, maybe we don't get it, or maybe we don't belong here—either way, we're weird, man." I included Jeremy in the "we" even though he had said nothing about "a goodly sum."

Jeremy responded, "No, your church is beautiful. It's just that this is a principle-driven conference for leaders of a principle-focused society."

Jeremy is brilliant, one of the most authentic men I know—by this I mean he is always Jeremy. He is a worshiper in every sense of the word. He only wants God's presence, and that desire influences all he touches. Before I met him, I think he talked less. He is one of those fellas who is a deep thinker but doesn't always feel the need to share his thoughts. Then we became friends. I really love sharing my thoughts. I'm a verbal processor. Plus, I am quite fond of my voice. Sometimes if I'm in an echo-ee bathroom I'll just start singing. It sounds really good. Over time, I think I wore Jeremy down, and now he often shares his thoughts just so I'll shut up.

"What do you mean?" I asked.

"Our leaders really don't need any more principles on how to grow a church." Jeremy had captured exactly what I was feeling.

This conference seemed to be a baptism in methods—full-on immersion for how to become a relevant church. There were booths on how to streamline Sunday morning with better PowerPoint, how to ensure better sound, how to get more people to your church through newsprint, Internet, TV, and radio. There were booths providing smoke machines and every kind of light imaginable, including lasers. There were business gurus, advertising gurus, "Feng shui" gurus, all available to help consult regarding building plans, media blitzes, and where best to place the coffee shops or bookstores. And of course there were endless how-to books as well; strategy guides for getting more "seats in the seats"—corny? Yeah, I know, there was probably a booth for that too.

None of the services being offered were wrong or even misplaced—I wholeheartedly believe in stratagem. I like light shows and good sound. I love coffee, especially in aesthetically pleasing environments, and I clearly love books. Please understand that I take no issue with the entrepreneurs who ran the booths. They had come to sell us what we want. It wasn't the supply that rubbed me wrong; it was the demand.

As I walked the halls I became heartsick. I wanted to throw over some tables, but thankfully I didn't. It all reminded me of a statistic I had heard some time before, which probably came from a book. Apparently 75 percent of the North American church believes the worship service is for them.[2] That is to say, they think worship is designed for their encouragement and for their well-being. That is very American. And it is absolutely false. However, this conference appeared to be catering to that deception.

I had not come to the conference to discover the principles of church growth. I had not come to be awed by a light show or entertained by a slick Coldplay cover. I had come in hopes of experiencing God's presence with the church leaders of tomorrow. I had come to discover how to be successful and relevant as a church leader, and I believed it was more about discovering His presence together and less about discovering the newest model of laser lights.

I love Coldplay *and* lasers, but they have nothing to do with relevant.

Jeremy's assessment was correct. We live in a principle-driven, principle-focused society. Knowledge and entertainment are the two primary pursuits of our consumer culture. I know from my years as a pastor the pressure to cater to need and expectation and call it ministry. But I have learned that ministry isn't about meeting people's expectations or needs, it's about providing opportunity for them to meet with Him. Principles are helpful but they won't redeem, restore, or save us. The best message and most spectacular lightshow won't heal a broken heart or redeem a fallen mind. It's revelation of His good love, it's the encounter, it's personal friendship with our Creator that satisfies our souls and makes us whole.

I remember many years ago, after leading worship on a Sunday morning, being approached by one of the church members. He told me he loved it when I led worship, and then he went on to say how on this particular day the worship service hadn't done anything for him. He was unmoved. I smiled and in my kindest voice said, "It wasn't my primary intention to move you." I don't worship to meet a need, I worship to discover and reveal the One who truly meets every need.

This fella wasn't the last to try and define success or determine relevance for me. But I am convinced that relevance is only experienced and revealed by being in God's presence—in the discovery of who He is. God *is* life. He *is* Love, He *is* Truth, and He defines relevant. To the depths that we respond and experience Him, we live, love, and know freedom, and we become like Him—we become relevant.

There is nothing wrong with learning how to do church better, but my heart longs to experience His presence and then discover *why* we are the church. My soul yearns for more—I want God encounters and I want to experience the miraculous wonders of living from His presence. I was born to define relevant. And so were you.

All creation is waiting for the church, you and me, to reveal what relevant truly is. They are waiting for us to live like Jesus, to become the walking, talking opportunity for experiencing His always-good love. We owe them an encounter. We owe them the true definition of relevant.

Relevant

Its the cry of my heart, my King,
That I'd display Your majesty

Jesus was relevant. He was relevant for one reason, and one reason only: He was in the Father and the Father was in Him. Jesus only did what He saw the Father do and He only said what He heard the Father say. He lived daily in His Father's presence. His worship is what defined relevant. And Jesus defined relevant His whole life. All thirty-three years of it.

Jesus defined relevant when He was born in a manger, and as a child, a youth, and a carpenter's son. He defined relevant when only a handful of people knew who He was. He defined relevant when thousands followed Him, hanging on His every word. When He healed the sick, when He raised the dead, when He fed hungry people, He was defining relevant. And the same was true when He ate with sinners and forgave the woman caught in adultery. He defined relevant when He walked on water and set people free.

And Jesus defined relevant when He told the masses that in order to be saved they would have to eat His flesh and drink His blood (see John 6). He defined relevant when all but His twelve disciples left Him. He defined relevant when He went to the temple with a whip and threw over some tables. When He stood before Herod, when He was beaten and hung on a cross, when He died, and again when He rose, each and every time He was defining relevant. And not once was relevant defined by what He did; rather, it was defined by whom He was in and who was in Him.

We know we are relevant the moment we can say in our hearts, "I am in the Father and the Father is in me." We know we are relevant the moment the next statement is true: "Anyone who has seen me has seen my Father." You see, relevance is about becoming one with Him (see John 17:21), about discovering His presence, about a worship lifestyle.

Yes, it will look like the miraculous; yes, it will look like hiddenness; and yes, it will look like misunderstanding. It will look like thousands of followers, and it will also look like no one following, except maybe a few sweet children who want to see the lion in the backyard.

And yes, relevant will look like suffering and dying. And yes, relevant will look like resurrection life. And all along the way it will set people free, invite revelation, and empower transformation. All along the way we will know success, not a success determined by this world, not a success determined by attendance numbers or lasers, but a success determined by His daily presence.

Hunger

Draw me to my knees, Lord
Make me hungry for more

Years ago, during a trip to Africa, I led a song called "Hungry" at a Christian high school. The chorus goes, "We are hungry for more of You." At first the students thought this an odd expression. But when I explained how we as believers could have an almost physical type of hunger for God's presence in our hearts, they responded by singing with a grasp of the word that astonished and humbled me. They had a greater understanding and experience of the word than I will probably ever know. They had revelation regarding the word *hunger*. Their hunger stirred my hunger that night, and the presence of God was real and sweet.

We experienced such a sense of awe and wonder at God's goodness. We knew He loved us powerfully and completely. There is nothing quite like a greater revelation of God's love, a greater awareness of His presence. We worshiped for hours but it felt like mere minutes.

Matthew 5:6 says, *"Blessed are those who hunger and thirst for righteousness, for they will be filled."* This Scripture promises a God encounter to those who hunger and thirst after God. This Scripture describes hunger as the catalyst to encounter the fullness of God.

I have discovered over the years that God will always respond to sincere hunger. He will come when we ask, and He will fill us with Himself. And that's what I want! I want a greater revelation of God's always-good love. I want to know the Father like Jesus knew the Father. I want to walk in the Spirit like Jesus walked in the Spirit. I want more and more of God. I want to be hungry—that I would be filled.

Do you know the saying, "We are what we eat"? Well, it could be said like this as well: "What we are hungry for determines what we eat." Amazingly, when it comes to a greater awareness of God's presence—the fullness of His love—the more we eat, the greater our hunger.

I've heard it said this way: in the natural we eat to get full, but in the spiritual we eat to get hungry. I am learning God loves filling us up while at the same time increasing our capacity for more. I am also learning it's our hunger that defines us, and what we are hungry for will determine our relevance.

Healing for Idiots

I'll live fully to the very end,
Without You it's a chasing of the winds

Jesus healed several blind men over the course of His last three years of ministry. And He never did it exactly the same way twice. I'm convinced He healed each of them differently for one reason: that's how His Father wanted it done.

Jesus displayed the mysterious adventure of living in the Father. He revealed a life guided by the Holy Spirit. He displayed an intimate faith, a worship lifestyle, a life of untamed surrender. And everything He did revealed relevance.

But if there was a second reason Jesus healed blind eyes differently, it was probably that He didn't want any formulaic principle-based books written on how to heal blind people, no best sellers titled *Healing for Idiots* that could later be sold in large quantity at conferences to folks so intent on chasing relevant they lost the point.

If Jesus had healed the same way every time, we might be tempted to take our eyes off Him and ferret out a principle. The greater works life isn't experienced because we know how to implement a principle from a book, even *the* Book. It's experienced through relationship, a daily revelation of Father, Son, and Holy Spirit.

Jesus showed us what it looks like to be in the Father. In the last three years of His ministry, He revealed mercy and grace and hope and trust and joy and peace and love. And all of these wonders, all these truths, are accessible for our own experience through revelation, intimate knowledge, firsthand experience, daily communion with Father, Son, and Holy Spirit.

To heal a blind man (from *Healing for Idiots*), taken from John 9:1-6:

- Discuss with those around you whether his sins or those of his parents caused his blindness. This should be done in a public place loud enough for the blind man to overhear you. You shouldn't have to talk too loud due to his hearing being enhanced on account of his blindness.

- Spit in the dirt. It must be a good amount of spit. You may also want a cup of water close at hand because this much spitting can cause dryness of mouth.

- Stir the spit and dust to a paste-like consistency, making sure you have a good amount of mud— about a palm full or the size of a baby's fist.

- Gently rub the mud upon the blind man's eyes. Note: Let him know what you are about to do so as not to spook him. Also, warn him it might sting a little.

- Smooth out the mud, and then tell the man to go to the well of Siloam. Don't help him get there and don't give him directions; if he wants to get healed, he'll figure it out on his own.

- Inform him he must wash in this river. WARNING: At no point do you tell him this will result in him getting his sight. But wink at him when no one's looking so he knows the odds are in his favor.

A Mystical God

It's Your heart I'm after
If I sought to capture
Would my pursuit be that of a fool

I love holding Karen's hand on almost any occasion. I believe it's one of the reasons a person gets married. It's a quiet celebration of love, a sincere expression of forever. Like when you're on a long road trip and suddenly you feel this overwhelming love for the girl next to you and you reach over and put your hand on hers and she knows…or when you are at the hospital waiting to hear some potentially scary news and she reaches over and takes your hand and you know…or when we've had a fight and it's over and we go for a walk and hold hands and we both know…yeah, sweeter than tupelo honey.

I also love holding my kids' hands. When we walk through the park or cross the street or pray. When we dance in private at home or when I tell them they have to hold my hand while we are in the glass store or the pottery store or the knife store. But that's it, that's where my handholding enjoyment ends.

I can tolerate old ladies' hands if we are greeting each other and they don't hold mine for too long. However, I dislike holding hands with the rest of you people, especially strangers. This is a problem when you grow up in the church. It seems that most pastors don't truly feel they have successfully conducted a service until we have all taken the hand of the person next to us. And inevitably the second I am forced to hold someone else's hand, my hands get sweaty and I suddenly develop muscle spasms. Or my ankle itches. I mean, it really itches. So I let go of the person's hand to scratch my ankle, and as soon as I take the person's hand again, my nose itches.

Plus when going in for the grip, should I go underhand or do I go over? It feels girly to grip overhand. What if I'm overhand with a girl? Then we are both uncomfortable. Of course sitting next to a girl is better than some of the other options. I once sat next to this old man who was in the middle of dabbing a perpetually running nose when the handholding unity part of the service came. He didn't even put the handkerchief back into his pocket. While still holding the kerchief, he reached out and grabbed my hand.

Speaking of handholding…

Years ago I read an interview with a well-known pastor of a large church. He told a story about going out to look at a piece of property with the elders of the church. They believed the property was to be the place where they were to build a new sanctuary. One of the elders said, "Let's hold hands and claim this property." The pastor, who is a logical kind of fella, said in the interview, it hadn't occurred to him to hold hands and pray that way. He probably doesn't like handholding either. He went on to say he's not wired like that—he's not the "mystical type."

"Amen, brother," I thought. "I'm not wired that way either." But it really wasn't the handholding part of the article that got me; it was the comment he made about not being mystical.

The word *mystical* caught my attention, because another well-known and respected pastor friend of mine had used it recently. We had been discussing how God seems to be moving in our country today. I told him a story about a miracle that God had recently orchestrated in my life. As soon as the word *miracle* was used, he shut the conversation down. He told me he was not a mystical sort of person. To him, in regard to the church, emotionalism and coincidence were more likely than a mystical God. He went on to say he had seen church leaders abuse the idea of the "mystical God" to get what they wanted.

That's fair. I completely understand his position. I too have met my share of fruitcakes who used "thus saith the Lord" to make up for a lack of character. I have seen leaders manipulate people by using the "mystical God." I have also watched people make life decisions ruled by their emotions instead of trust. I am a logical person. If a black cat crosses my path, it's just a black cat. If it happens again, it's a coincidence. I'm not superstitious and my reserved personality doesn't tend to put much stock in the mystical.

But the problem is, God *is* mystical. *Mystical* means- "of or having a spiritual reality or import not apparent to the intelligence, mysterious."[3] I don't know about you, but the God in my life often fits that description. He is not always logical; at least not in the way I understand it. There also appears to be no such thing as coincidence with God. No accidents and no surprises. His love, mercy, grace, and goodness are all beyond comprehension.

Here is the scary but awesome thing. If we fully surrender our lives to this mysterious God, He will invite us to go places with Him that might even offend the mind. But oh, the things we'll see! Oh, the life we will live! We might even see and experience "greater things" than Jesus saw and experienced.

The Most Practical Mystic on the Planet

When Jesus looked up and saw a great crowd coming toward Him, He said to Philip, "Where shall we buy bread for these people to eat?" He asked this only to test him, for He already had in mind what He was going to do. Philip answered Him, "Eight months' wages would not buy enough bread for each one to have a bite!" Another of His disciples, Andrew, Simon Peter's brother, spoke up, "Here is a boy with five small barley loaves and two small fish, but how far will they go among so many?" (John 6:5-9)

Jesus, always in the Father, assesses the situation. "The people are hungry. How much food do we have?" He is practical. However, His approach regarding the solution was absolutely mystical. He supernaturally multiplied five small barley loaves and two small fish. And everyone there got to eat that day.

If we were to look at this situation outside of the Father, the practical solution would either be to send the people home or get religious, apply a principle, and call for a fast. But when Jesus displayed the Kingdom and revealed His Father's heart, it looked like the miraculous, like the mystical; once again He defined relevant. The funny thing is that Jesus was the most practical person within 100,000 miles of this situation—what's more practical than multiplying the food? I want to know this kind of relevant, I want this kind of success, and I want these stories to be my stories.

Do you realize that when Jesus takes a head count, it's never to prove He is relevant; it's always to reveal the mystical, mysterious, miraculous goodness of His Father's love. He doesn't need more Twitter followers or likes on Facebook to be relevant, He defines it with the power of His presence—in the perfection of His love.

Could you imagine if we, the church, experienced these kinds of miracles on a regular basis? Could you imagine what would happen if we could reveal the goodness of our Father by miraculously meeting the needs of a lost and dying world? Now throw in a Coldplay cover and some laser lights—we'd be unstoppable!

Here's the deal: our Father loves to move outside of our ability to understand and into the mysterious in order to practically provide for us. We just need to be willing to say yes to the mystical goodness of His presence, even when we have to do something silly or uncomfortable like praying for that stranger, or giving beyond comfortable, or believing when it's impossible, or holding the hand of the old guy next to us—though I would like to note there was no mention of handholding in the fish and loaves miracle.

I want to be willing to embrace all of God. I'm up for it. And I'm up for it for two reasons—first, I want the experience, the story; and second, I want an expanded understanding regarding God, the revelation.

I spent several miserably dull years never allowing God to operate in the mysterious, and I'm never going back there again. I am not interested in principles without the mystery of His presence. I have decided to fully embrace all of my promise, and that means I must fully embrace all of God. That includes the God who fed thousands of people with five barley loaves and two fish.

I would much rather move forward into the unknown with a good, powerful, mystical God than live in the now with a packaged, distant, impotent God. I want the wonder of His presence in my every breath. And I am willing to risk looking foolish, acting stupid, and appearing irrelevant in my pursuit of my miracle-working best friend, Jesus.

It's Our Worship that Defines Relevant

Looking down I see my feet
Where once I feared to walk

David steps out onto the battlefield to face Goliath, and I can't help but wonder what the Israelite men on the sidelines were thinking. We know there were some—in particular, David's own brothers—who thought it was none of his business, he did not belong there, he should keep his mouth shut, and he should stay out of the way. Many of the men, I imagine, were angry and probably had thoughts like, "Who does this kid think he is?" and maybe even, "Cocky kid. He deserves what's coming."

Yet I have to believe—I *must* believe—there were some who knew, the moment they saw it, the rightness of it, the righteousness of it. I have to believe there were some who watched David take the field and wished they had been the one to step out. I have to believe with some the heart was whispering yes even when the mind screamed no. And I do believe this because I have been that man. I have watched while others embraced their promise with a revelation of God and defiance toward logic. I have watched and my spirit has leapt within me and said, "Me too!"

David's actions appeared absolutely irrelevant regarding the outcome of the battle before Goliath fell. He was a fool, he was countercultural, he was crazy, he was irrelevant. And then the giant fell, and suddenly there was no one more relevant than David. He stepped onto the field of battle, radically surrendered his will, his comfort, even his life, to the Promise Giver. His actions spoke volumes: "I serve a *mystical God* and I am living in a spiritual reality not apparent to the intelligence. I am living from His presence, I am intimate with His goodness, and He will be exalted above all else." David committed an amazing act of worship: he responded in trust by giving all of himself, and his worship defined relevant.

I believe the measure of our relevance is directly related to the measure of our worship. I'm not just referring to worship in song, but I'm referring to an untamed lifestyle of radical surrender. Worship is the response of a heart that knows love—it's birthed from relationship. And the greater our revelation of His love, the more radical our worship, until we find ourselves squaring off against giants and defining relevant.

What's amazing is that when worship is witnessed at such a level, it commands a response. True worshipers will make those around them hungry, nervous, or even angry. True worshipers will force those around them to radically surrender and join in or get out of the game. And a worship lifestyle radically impacts and defines the world we live in.

Everything in the Kingdom of God is birthed out of worship, out of response to the goodness of God. All of our promises are embraced through worship. It is an act of surrender, our will found in God's. But our worship doesn't stop at surrender. When we surrender to God, He invites us into the mystical that is the "untamed." This is a place where we can demonstrate our worship. Show and tell. And as David demonstrated, when surrender proceeds untamed, our promise is engaged and expanded, and the Kingdom is always advanced—victory is always the result. And when everyone gets to partake of your personal victory, I would say that's pretty relevant.

When a person enters into this kind of radical worship, giants die. In this case, David's worship not only brought him personal victory, but it brought a victory everyone partook of. It brought strength to a nation. Because of David's radical act of worship, the Israelites won the day. This kind of worship engages a personal promise and therefore expands the parameters of the Kingdom. This kind of worship is what we are called to. Worship that starts with surrender but doesn't end there, the kind of worship that thrusts us wildly into defining relevant.

Revelation, Greater Works, and Relevant

Please be all I need, please, my heart cries, please be all I need
If life were a song, come, Savior, come, sing in me...a beautiful song

Jesus says in John 14:10-11, *"Don't you believe that I am in the Father, and that the Father is in Me? The words I say to you are not just My own. Rather, it is the Father, living in Me, who is doing His work. Believe Me when I say that I am in the Father and the Father is in Me; or at least believe on the evidence of the miracles themselves."* Earlier in John He actually says, *"Do not believe me unless I do what My Father does"* (John 10:37).

Jesus revealed that while the definition of relevant was being one with the Father, the expression of relevant was miracles. What's more, He actually said we didn't have to believe in Him if He didn't do miracles. And do you know what the very next verse says? *"But if I do it, even though you do not believe Me, believe the miracles, that you may know and understand that the Father is in Me, and I in the Father"* (John 10:38). I believe Jesus's life reveals that when we are one with the Father, we become the expression of His will here on earth, and that looks like the miraculous, and it defines relevance.

You and I are meant to define relevant—to know the Father and, like Jesus, reveal Him to our family, our coworkers, and our neighbors through a "greater works than these" worship lifestyle. I believe that to truly define relevant to the world, we must have our own revelation of God. We must be willing to risk chasing a revolutionary God. We must be crazy enough to trust and obey, willing to fail, and yet still expect to succeed. We need our own God encounters, our own God stories. Oh, by the way, this type of surrendered and untamed living? It looks like the "mystical."

I want to live this life in the brilliance of Your song
I want to worship You with a life fully sung...a beautiful song

Endnotes

1.   "The Beautiful Letdown," Switchfoot, *The Beautiful Letdown*, Sony Music Entertainment, 2003.

2.   George Barna, *Revolution* (Carol Stream, IL: Tyndale, 2005).

3.   American Heritage Dictionary, s.v. "mystical."

Chapter 8

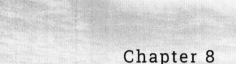

Surrendered and Untamed

The Story, Part 1—The God Encounter

I'm consumed 'neath heaven's crush
You are here and You're glorious

I have had several encounters with God throughout my life, times where I knew without any doubt He was in the room. Two weeks after arriving in North Carolina, I had one of those moments. I found myself facedown on my living room floor. I prayed like David in Psalm 139:23. I asked my Father to search me, to know me. I invited His presence to come, and I asked for greater revelation.

There are some who would say God is always with us and there is no need to ask for more of Him. But even Jesus experienced moments of greater revelation. At Jesus's baptism, for example, His Father spoke from heaven and the Holy Spirit descended in the form of a dove. And on the Mount of Transfiguration, Jesus experienced His Father's presence in such a profound way that His face shone like the sun and His clothing was white like lightning.

You know, God is a respecter of persons. He will never force Himself on us. Surrender is always voluntary. He will always wait for the invitation. It's not that He doesn't already know us; He can give a number to the hairs on our heads. But when it comes to an intimate relationship with God, He waits for an invitation. This is because intimacy takes two people. If we don't invite Him to know us just as He has invited us to know Him, we will never experience closeness.

So that night, with my invitation, He made His presence known in a profound way. His power was manifest in the room—that is to say, I couldn't move. I felt His presence physically. Talk about a mystical experience. I lay on the floor as the goodness of His presence filled the room. He was undeniably God. This was a "burning bush" moment in my life (see Exod. 3).

During this time, my Father poured out His heart of love for me and restored my soul. And, as always in these encounters, He cemented His promise in my heart. All I could do was love Him more. All I could do was respond to and worship Him.

After an hour or so, we began to talk like old friends. I spoke out loud and He responded to my heart. It was a wonderfully prolonged time where we expressed our love for each other. I know this may sound crazy to some, but this kind of thing happened in the Bible, right? Consider when Moses met God at the burning bush or when the disciples experienced the Holy Spirit in the upper room shortly after Jesus ascended to heaven.

As the night progressed, I began to ask questions about what Karen and I would face in the days ahead. We had just moved to a new city to work with a new ministry without any guarantee of a paycheck, so I was particularly interested in how I was to provide for my family.

There was a moment when I felt like God responded to my questions with one of His own: "Do you trust Me?" I have since learned this is a question God will ask every believer who desires to live a good story. This question must be answered time and again as we engage our promise. I responded the only way a believer can: "Yes, Father, I trust You."

I felt God respond to my heart immediately, saying, "Then stay the course and believe." He gave me a few more specifics and then asked me to get up and write them down. I did and then spent the rest of the night worshiping Him. I felt my Father assure me He was good and His provision would neither be a day early or a day late. He felt as close to me as my own skin that night.

The next morning I shared with Karen all that had happened. Karen and I had moved to North Carolina out of obedience, and so with the word from our Father we decided together that, regardless of our circumstances, we would stay the course and believe.

There is a saying that, "God is rarely early, but He is never late." We've since changed it to "God is rarely early and...well, He is rarely early."

The Jump

I was born to bring You glory, I was born to sing Your fame
From my hilltop to my valley I'm surrendered and untamed

I have a friend named Joel Carver. I just call him Carver for short. I think Carver is a pretty cool name, but that's beside the point. He is the kind of guy who just knows how to have fun, and he's not scared of anything. I know this because every time we talk about doing something fun and scary, he always says, "I'm not scared."

I had gone to Seattle to surprise my friend Carver for his birthday. His wife, Tennille, Karen, and I had planned the surprise for months beforehand. So when I showed up out of the blue, it didn't take long for both of us to decide we needed to do something amazing to mark this special occasion. After a brief discussion, that "something" was obvious—tandem skydiving.

The day before we jumped, I was a nervous wreck. Any time I thought about it, I got queasy. Carver and I began to relate stories we had heard of other jumpers, and, of course, eventually the talk turned to the horror stories until one of us would laugh nervously. Then Carver would give his famous phrase, "I'm not scared." Then we'd change the subject.

But once we arrived at the small shack out in the beautiful Northwest countryside, my feelings turned from nervous to excited. As I signed the forms that essentially said, "If you die, or are terribly injured, we are sorry but you can't blame us because you're the idiot who wanted to jump out of an airplane in the first place," I wasn't nervous. As I put on the orange prisonlike jumpsuit, and my instructor strapped on my harness, I wasn't scared. In fact, I was giddy, joking, and tee-hee-ing with Carver like an adolescent schoolgirl.

On the van ride over to the plane, I was practically humming with anticipation. And as I stood on the tarmac, I listened with a sense of exhilaration as my instructor ran through the last-minute details. When he mentioned the importance of keeping our arms and legs close to our body so they wouldn't act as a windmill causing us to spin out of control, I fearlessly joked how we had nicknamed that phenomenon "the death spin."

For those who do not know, there have been times when a jumper begins to spin so violently they lose control of their senses. They can begin to experience euphoria to such an extent they actually lose track of time—when jumping out of an airplane, losing track of time is always a bad idea. They have actually found jumpers (landers?) with unpulled parachutes, which is probably where that joke came from: "Parachute for sale, never been opened, small bloodstain."

When the eight of us climbed into the Volkswagen bug with wings, I was grinning from ear to ear. As we neared the end of the runway, I thought excitedly, "Here we go!" The second we left earth, however, I experienced a terror beyond words. Honestly, if there had not been a girl on the plane, I may have lost control of my bladder. I'm not saying I did pee myself, I'm just saying I may have if not for that girl.

It was a windy day and the takeoff was turbulent. The earth disappeared beneath us at an alarming rate. I remember being consumed with two thoughts—first, "Is there any way I can get out of this?" and then, "Oh $%@&, the death spin." Still, I'm proud to say I manned up and you couldn't see the terror on my face or hear it in my voice.

If the takeoff was traumatic, when the instructor told Carver and I to roll up the flimsy canvas flap that separated us from 11,000 feet of sky, I nearly had a seizure. At this point I vaguely remember my instructor pointing out the beautiful landscape below us. "Look at the mountains! Aren't they beautiful?"

To which I responded, "Yeah, they are gorgeous." But I couldn't see a thing.

My instructor kept yapping. "Look at the Seattle skyline, and the ocean, isn't it all amazing?"

"Shut up, just shut your mouth!" I wanted to scream. But instead I graciously said, "Yeah, it's all amazing." Still, I couldn't see squat.

Then the plane slowed down and my instructor told me to swing my feet out over the nothingness. "That's the dumbest thing I've ever heard. You are an idiot!" I thought to myself. But I robotically obeyed as I white-knuckled a bar on the inside of the plane. I remember hysterically grasping the irony of holding this bar to keep me from falling out when at any moment we were going to jump. Irony is always so ironic.

At this point my mind had exhausted every scenario in which I could get out of jumping and still retain my dignity. "What if the plane were to run out of gas?" I thought. "No, wait, that's not a good idea. What if I faked a seizure—that's it! Great idea, Jason. No, wait... the fastest way to a hospital is what I'm trying to avoid. What if...."

But no matter how hard I tried, I couldn't find a plausible way out of jumping. It was gonna happen!

Then the pilot shouted, "We missed the drop. I'll take us around again!" The plane tilted, and for about five minutes I had to sit at the edge looking down at my toes, which at this point hung 11,000 feet over earth.

For the first minute I was in full panic. I started to wonder about my tandem instructor. I realized I didn't know anything about him. I should have asked him some personal questions, like, "How is your home life?" or "Have you been feeling depressed lately?" I was pretty sure it wasn't my time to check out, but I had no idea about my tandem instructor. I pictured myself in heaven, and Jesus asking, "What are you doing here?" "I'm with him," I would say, as I pointed at my instructor.

Plus, were we really strapped together? I mean, I was laughing about the death spin when he did that, so I think I felt it. I was 99 percent sure. No wait, 97 percent sure…92 percent sure… Well, you get the picture. I kept looking inside the plane at Carver and subtly pointing to my straps. But he didn't understand and I didn't want to yell as I thought now was not the best time to upset my tandem instructor by questioning his competence.

Clearly I was losing it. Then Carver yelled, "Surrendered and untamed, baby!" And something happened—it was like scales fell from my eyes. I took a deep breath and began to praise God. At that moment I experienced a peace absolutely at odds with my circumstance. Maybe even a peace that surpasses understanding. There on the edge of my demise, I worshiped. I realized this was something I had dreamed of doing my entire life. Here I was, 11,000 feet above earth, and even though I was terrified, there was peace. And it was then I saw the beautiful mountains, the ocean, and the skyline.

My tandem instructor tapped my shoulder and we rocked back and forth once, twice—and suddenly I was skydiving. Surrendered and untamed, baby!

The Story, Part 2—Do Not Strike the Rock

I climbed the mountain and got on my knees
Until revival made a home inside of me

You remember the God encounter I talked about earlier, right? Well, after that night, Karen and I began to live financially by faith. Most of my time was spent helping grow the ministry God had called us to, a young ministry unable to provide for us financially. But God had already made it clear I was to believe and stay the course, and He would provide. "Not a day early or a day late," He'd said. I paid more attention to the second part of His statement, but He was serious about both.

Not that I wasn't taking odd jobs, but as strange as this may sound, I wasn't pursuing extra work during this season. In fact, this was probably the hardest battle I faced as day in and day out I watched our money disappear and yet I felt no release from God to fix it. This opposed all I understood about work and providing for my family. Before this season, if someone had told me they were broke but they didn't have a paying job and were not even looking for one, I would have kindly told them to get off their butt and go find one. As you can imagine, I was in agony.

One day while driving by a Home Depot and crying out to God for provision, I said, "That's it, Father, I'm going in there and I'm getting a job." Immediately my Father spoke to my heart saying, "Do not strike the rock." It was a reference to Moses, who out of frustration acted without the word from God and it cost him the Promised Land. "Then how do I pay my mortgage?" I asked as I began to weep in frustration.

I felt what my Father was asking of me was absolutely insane and irresponsible. I was constantly fighting deep insecurities around others, particularly church leaders and family as they all had some idea regarding my financial situation and that I wasn't actively seeking a paying gig. I felt like a fool, like an absolute loser; worse, I wrestled with the idea that I was being lazy and worried that those around me thought I was being lazy as well. I remember sitting with a pastor as he implored me to go get a job. "Aren't you doing anything?" he asked. Another pastor whom I highly respected gave me this Scripture: "A man who can't provide for his family is worse than an infidel" (see 1 Tim. 5:8). Ah, pastoral care. The definition of infidel is "unbeliever," which was the opposite of what I was going for.

The sheer agony for me during this season came from the fact that, in theory, I agreed with these pastors and the truths in those Scriptures. Yet I had heard my Father speak to my heart—"stay the course and believe"—and this just didn't allow for me to step away from what He had asked of me and what He had promised.

I guess what I'm trying to say is this: while I was chasing obedience, while I was living with an intentional yes in my heart, my experience of God was conflicting with my current understanding of Him. This passage below, which is taken from my journal, was written during that season:

> *I'm desperate, Lord, for You to move on my behalf. I'm guilty and sick, my prayers an old story told too many times. I'm humbled by my need. Those around me think I'm a lazy fool and that You never talk to me. I must see You move or I will die. I'm desperate but still I will endeavor not to be discouraged. I'm hoping and believing, "**because Your love is meteoric, Your loyalty astronomic**" (Psalm 36:5-6 MSG).*

However, at the same time I was experiencing all these insecurities, I was also experiencing my Father's presence in a day-by-day, hour-by-hour way. I knew He was pleased with me; He reminded me of this regularly. I often heard Him echo what He said to Jesus, "I love you, son, and I am well pleased with you." I can tell you from experience: when you know your heavenly Father is pleased, you can take another step.

I've gotta tell you, looking back, this season holds some of Jason and Karen Clark's sweetest memories. There was an amazing peace in our home. At night I would walk through the house and look in on my sleeping kids, and the fear of not knowing where they would sleep if we lost the house would begin to assault me. Then just as quick I would give it back to my Father: "These are Your kids too."

I would then go downstairs and make myself some coffee and I would pour a mug for Jesus as well. Then I would go into my living room and sit down in my favorite chair. I would put Jesus's mug out on the coffee table and then I would put mine down. You may think I'm a little odd—and I probably am—but it's not that I expected Jesus to drink the coffee. That wasn't the point. When you are facing seemingly insurmountable obstacles because of obedience, you *want* to know God is there, you *need* to experience His presence. Pouring Him a mug of coffee was simply my way of letting my Father know I was after an intimate relationship with Him.

Once I was settled, I would close my eyes and begin to thank Him. His presence in the form of peace would come, I would feel His pleasure, His closeness, and it was so sweet. These were the moments when faith was restored. And I know you are wondering…He has yet to drink the coffee.

If you are in the center of God's will, even though a season may be difficult, the peace of God that "passes all understanding" can still reign in your heart. In fact, you could say that to have access to this kind of peace, you have to be in a situation beyond your ability to understand.

There is a peace that comes with trusting and obeying—a supernatural ability to rest when encountering the overwhelming. Karen and I felt as though we were in the eye of the perfect storm. But as long as our focus remained on our Father, even though the chaos surrounded us, it never touched us, at least not in our hearts. That place was reserved for Jesus. It was as if we experienced what Jesus experienced when He slept in the boat through the storm. Shaken but not stirred.

For Karen and me, this was a season of the absolute unknown, but it was also incredibly fulfilling, as the revelation of God's love was never more profound, as His presence was never so close. For us, this was a journey of obedience in the face of insanity, and we chose to believe, we chose to obey, we chose to trust. The funny thing is, once you get to a certain point in your obedience, choice is almost irrelevant. There is a point of no return.

It's like this. Once you've jumped, there's no getting back in the plane. And to be honest, once you jump, faith in a parachute is irrelevant. It will work or it won't. Your faith no longer has any practical bearing on the outcome. And yet, it was faith in a parachute that got you there. So regardless of what you are feeling, the reality is that while hurtling toward earth, your faith in a parachute is the only thing that matters.

The Story, Part 3—Gratefulness

You've captured my heart, now I'm forever Yours
I give You all, all I am, Lord

When the propane ran out for the grill, we stopped grilling. I personally learned how to stitch but was still down to one pair of jeans. We had eBayed everything that wasn't nailed down, including all my recording gear. Our fridge was empty, and our pantry was close behind. When the vacuum broke, I vacuumed the house on my hands and knees with a tiny Shop-Vac. "Father, do You see this?" I would ask.

However, throughout this season we knew we were blessed. We chose to believe it and we chose to see it. While there is great need in this world, we can always find something to be grateful about. Karen and I were able to see His provision in the small things. Even though we were overwhelmed, we guarded our hearts against self-pity.

Self-pity is deadly. It will shred a believing heart in moments. Whenever Karen and I began to realize we were experiencing self-pity, we would decide to give thanks to God for all of His goodness, often even making a list of all He had done in and for us.

Gratefulness is the key to victory in the battle against self-pity. God is always good, so when we focus on His goodness it is impossible not to believe. Looking for evidences of His goodness in our lives and then giving thanks always increases our faith.

Self-pity cannot exist in the presence of gratefulness. I have seen this firsthand with my kids. We will be driving down the road after having gone out for pizza, after having gone to the swimming pool, after having gone to the theater, after having gone to the amusement park, after having gone jet skiing, after having flown on a space odyssey through the Dagobah system, when suddenly one of them will remember something we didn't get to do that day. Then they will begin to complain. It starts out with a statement like this: "We never have any fun," followed by a list of things they never get to do. The words "never" and "always" are used freely as one complaint after another is piled on until the minivan (I'm that cool) is filled with a cloud of self-pity.

That's when I bark, "Quiet!" Then, "I want five things from each of you that you are grateful for. Quick!" It starts out slowly as they can't seem to think of anything, so I remind them somewhat sarcastically, "Ahh, the Dagobah system?"

Eva, our youngest, likes this game and always gets there first. Finally Maddy remembers something and then Ethan follows close behind. A little more time and Maddy has something else, and a little more time and Ethan has found one more thing. By now Eva has given ten. At first the two oldest are paying close attention to how many things they have been grateful for, but by the time we get to number four, the atmosphere in the minivan has changed. And by the time we get to five, we just keep going until we are matching Eva. Eventually all we see is the goodness of God. There is no end of things we can be grateful for.

I told my kids the other day that joy is found in gratefulness, that contentment is discovered in thankfulness. Karen and I are learning to practice gratefulness, even when we're in the tough wilderness seasons—especially, when we're in the tough wilderness seasons. Karen and I are convinced that living thankful not only empowers us into joy and peace, but we reveal and empower a legacy of full life, health, and peace for our kids as well. We want to give them the road map to true happiness.

When we learn gratefulness, we begin to see God as He is. We also begin to see the fullness of what He has given us. In fact, His goodness will become so overwhelming that the desire to give even in the midst of need will overcome us. Therefore a grateful lifestyle will not just impact us but will have eternal significance to those with whom we come into contact. We can only give what we have, and gratefulness increases our awareness of how big God is and, in connection, how rich we truly are.

The Story, Part 4—Ketchup and a Plan

I have dreamed and still believe.
I have risked and I have lost.
But looking down I see my feet,
Where once I feared to walk

"Jesus, please let there be enough money on our credit card to buy this bottle of ketchup," I prayed. I was walking the grocery store aisle and I was in deep conversation with God. I repeated the prayer that had become my mantra over the last six months: "Father, I just want Your favor. I want Your presence. It doesn't matter what it looks like. I will do anything, just come and show me what Your favor on my life looks like."

It wasn't the first time I'd prayed that prayer, but it was the first "suddenly." Suddenly, as I pulled the bottle of ketchup off the shelf, I had a thought. As I absently walked the aisle it turned into a plan. Six months earlier my dad had invited Jeremy and myself into a new business venture. I had turned him down. I was not going to "put my hand to another plow" until I personally heard from God. I was done with good ideas if they were not God ideas. Second, in my mind, my promise looked nothing like what my dad had proposed.

Walking down that grocery store aisle, God gave me two things. First, He gave me a plan of action. Second, and more importantly, He gave me a green light. Suddenly I felt an overwhelming excitement to pursue this business. Where six months earlier I would have felt sick at the idea, I was now passionate about it. That night Karen and I prayed about it and then we decided to step out and start the company.

Only Dead Men Can Go

A perfect fear came and claimed my soul
Said this is a place only dead men can go

Jeremy was precise, his newest victims already forgotten. He was moving forward again yelling instructions. We had the flag in our sights now. I barked at the two kids in front of me as paint whizzed past my head. "Over there, pin them down." I flanked around and delivered the perfect head shot, my last shot. I was out of ammo.

The kid to my left, one of ours, went down. "I'm hit, I'm hit," he screamed. Then to my right, "Hit, I'm out!" It was chaos. With my back against a downed tree, I whisper-yelled over to Jeremy, "I'm out of ammo." He nodded. "Me too." He was crouched behind an old tire.

And there it was, our moment of genius. "Shock and Awe"— except it was more like "Bluff and Bluster." We, the only two players left on our team, out of ammo, ran like lunatics straight for the flag, dry firing our weapons all the way. We knew we were "dead men" either way, so we decided to go out on offense. I'm proud to report we were touched by the paintball gods that day and captured the flag without being shot. We won. This story is one of the greats and will be forever preserved in the annals of paintball history.

In his book *Uprising*, Erwin McManus describes a place where only dead men can go. In fact, I wrote a song by the same title. Besides the lyrical poetry, the essence of what he described grabbed me at a deeper gut level. Have you ever read something that just jumped out at you, something you knew was truth but didn't fully grasp yet?

God wants to take us to places that will require total surrender. God wants to take us to places that will require us to take risks, to look the fool, and to do it with as much believing as we can possess. God wants to take us to a place that requires us to offer up our very lives so we might meet Him and know Him there. There really are some places only dead men can go.

The Story, Part 5—Salvation

I believe it's begun and is finished, a revolution of the cross
I've awakened to a movement, love my burden,
the birthplace of holiness

It was Friday. On Monday the gas was to be turned off, Wednesday the electric, and Thursday the water. We were not just slightly overdue on these bills—we were months behind. We had turned our bedroom phone ringer off because our morning wakeup call was generally a bill collector. Our credit was maxed out and all of our natural resources were used up except one, our SUV, which had been in the paper for two months. Though a year earlier God had promised me that regarding our finances He would provide for us "not a day early or a day late," in all honesty God seemed late. We were afraid. Afraid we'd lose our house, afraid we had missed it, afraid we looked like fools.

On Friday I remember telling my dad, "We can now see the whites of the giant's eyes." That was pretty much all we could see. We were at the point of no return. We had committed everything we had and there was no going back. And that's where we found ourselves... like David, a mere boy standing on the battlefield, armed only with a strip of leather and a stone, in front of a demon of a man.

When you find yourself in this circumstance and you are there because you chased obedience, you said yes time and again, there is nothing left for you to do but yell real loud, run at the giant, and sling the stone. For us, in a sense, believing almost seemed irrelevant; there was either going to be a miracle or the giant was going to skewer us. But Karen and I again decided we would go into the weekend believing.

I received a phone call on Saturday: "Is your Honda still for sale?"

"Yes," I said.

"Great, I'm on my way."

A guy shows up with cash and buys our SUV. On Monday we paid all of our immediate bills. We even bought a little propane and had a cookout celebration. With the rest of the money, I invested in the business plan God had given Jeremy, my dad, and me. Within a month the business was paying my bills, it doubled the second month, and again the third and fourth month. Within six months it was providing for three families. It truly was a miracle.

For the Joy Set before *Us*

Come, let's know our Savior's journey
And find our story in His song

Just before God released His miracle, I met with one of my closest friends, Shawn Ring, over Chinese. Ring is one of the most successful believers I know, and by this I mean he is successful at believing. He could stand down an army of murderous stormtroopers with a toothpick if God asked him to. I have truly seen him in some incredibly hard situations and marveled at his faith.

"Well, we are pretty desperate," I told him one day, depressed. "We are pretty close to dead." I went on to tell him the state of things, how we had done everything God had asked us to do, that we were walking in obedience, risking all to follow Him, and yet we were still in bad shape. Or as I put it, we were "dying." I was feeling a little sorry for myself.

Ring started laughing, his eyes twinkling mischievously. He leaned back in his chair and said, "Well, there's one thing you've excelled at, bro."

"What's that?" I was slightly annoyed.

With a grin he said, "You've been pretty good at dying."

After I punched him I realized what he said was a compliment.

What Ring was saying is there are two ways to die: you can either die believing or you can die in unbelief. There is a Scripture in Romans that says, *"And we know that all things work together for good to those who love God, to those who are the called according to His purpose"* (Rom. 8:28 NKJV). So you can either die believing God is good and He will work even your death to your good, or you can die in disappointment, doubt, and unbelief.

Jesus knew He was to die, to suffer miserably, to be humiliated, and spat upon. Did you know Jesus also knew that wasn't how His story was going to end? He even told people about it before He died. He knew He would rise from the dead.

Jesus knew the only way to salvation was through the cross. The only way to life was through death. And this is what amazes me. Jesus died violently, painfully, quietly, with grace and humility, but most of all, Jesus died believing. It was believing that took Him from the Last Supper to the garden, it was believing that took Him from the garden to the cross, believing He would rise three days later, that total salvation would be won for all time for all people. He knew the end of the story. And He died and rose again so we could know ours.

The author of Hebrews tells us:

> *Let us fix our eyes on Jesus, the author and perfecter of our faith, who for the joy set before Him endured the cross, scorning its shame, and sat down at the right hand of the throne of God* (Hebrews 12:2).

I want to make this clear: the cross is the foundation upon which our faith is built. Jesus is the cornerstone. But we have to know it wasn't Jesus's focal point. His focus was on what the cross bought for you and me—the opportunity to know our Father personally. Jesus's joy and focal point was on a relationship with you and me. The battle is not the point; the romance is the point.

What we must see is that the cross is the doorway to our destiny—it's the threshold to our future, the launching pad to our promise. It's the surrender that thrusts us into the untamed. Our salvation through the cross, although it is the most beautiful of God's miracles, is not the end of our story; it's where our story gets interesting, because it's the beginning of an untamed life.

If we embrace our promise, if we live a good story, we will experience cross situations in our lives, but that isn't the end. The end of the story is the joy of greater intimacy with Father, Son, and Holy Spirit. It's the surrendered and untamed existence God has called us all to live. I am learning that during cross seasons in life, if I'm going to "die good," I have to shift my focus from the cross to the joy on the other side of the cross. In fact, it's that focus shift that empowers me to endure and believe during the cross seasons.

Even at the cross it's about believing. Maybe I should say, especially at the cross it's about believing. First Peter 1:9 says, *"Because you kept on believing, you'll get what you're looking forward to: total salvation"* (MSG). Total salvation is what we are after as believers. It is the fully alive way of life. It's the other side of the cross, understanding that our journey doesn't end at salvation—our journey is about resurrection life.

I love Jesus for the cross, and I especially love Him for resurrection life—the joy on the other side of the cross.

He showed us that when we find ourselves on *our* cross due to obedience, hanging on by a nail, so to speak, we must be doing something right. He showed us what it looks like to believe even unto death. And He showed us it's never about death; it's always about life. So keep believing, because only dead men can experience resurrection.

Surrendered and untamed, baby!

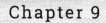

Chapter 9

Learning to Dance

The Lawn Mower

I know what you're hiding from
And I know where we're going to

Around the age of thirty, an awful realization began to gnaw at me. I fought it the best I could, but not with as much blind defiance as I had in my twenties. My realization was this: I may not be invincible. That thought first entered my consciousness after an incident with the lawn mower.

One hot Mississippi Saturday, I went out to mow the lawn. The lawn mower was giving me fits and I began to pull the cord like I was sixteen. And I pulled my arm out of its socket. I fell to the driveway and began rolling around in agony. No matter how I squirmed, I couldn't get my arm to go back in. Grunting and gasping, I could only think of Mel Gibson and the Lethal Weapon movies. In those cinematic classics, Mel Gibson's character was constantly pulling his arm out of socket and it was humorous and very entertaining to watch him as he struggled to put it back in. I remembered in one of the movies he put his arm back in its socket by slamming his shoulder against a wall.

With that memory as my only reference for solving a dislocated arm, I half crawled, half rolled over to the open garage door. Panting and sweating with the pain, I crawled up the doorframe. Then, in between "God help me" and "s*&#," I slammed my arm against the doorframe. There was an excruciating pain as my arm popped back into its socket. Then an exhaled string of "Thank You, Fathers" as I leaned against the doorframe, thinking this wasn't that humorous or entertaining after all. I was reminded of that Bible verse about "the grass withereth," so I decided mowing is stupid.

As I turned, I saw my neighbor Jim standing in his driveway looking at me with a mix of sympathy and a smile. I grimaced back at him, realizing with some annoyance that apparently it is still humorous and entertaining. Then I waved with my good arm and said, "Hi, Jim," mumbled something about it being a beautiful day, and went inside thinking to myself, "Is this what happens when you get old?" and "Jim is a donkey, a real Balaam's ass."

This was the first day I realized that just maybe I'm not invincible. But all of this really only makes sense if I tell you about the triple black.

Triple Black Diamond

For Your glory, it's Your story working in me

About three years earlier, my whole family went to Colorado on a three-day family ski trip. The weather was beautiful, with lots of powder and a bright sun. Over the course of three days, I had the opportunity to ski with my sister, Aimee, my brother-in-law, Eric, and even Karen, as Mom watched our kids.

Mostly though, I skied with my brother Joel. Over those three days, we skied most of the mountain and nearly died a couple of times. At dusk on our last day, we stood at the edge of the triple black diamond. It was our last run of the night, the trip, and the year—so it had to be a good one. If you have never skied a triple black diamond run in Colorado, well, it's almost a religious experience. It's straight down, moguls the size of log cabins, grinning-like-a-fool kinda fun. It's absolutely exhilarating.

Joel and I have skied some amazing places, but by no means are we especially good. Yes, we were on the triple black diamond, but that was only because anyone *can* do a triple black diamond. There are no triple black diamond police at the top of the run looking for triple black diamond credentials. And Mom wasn't with us, so we skied it. Why? Because we *could.*

When Joel and I ski a triple black diamond, there is no grace or form; there is only survival. It isn't that we don't want to look sexy; it's just hard to do so when skiing beyond one's ability. Of course, that's half the fun—knowing you are in a little over your head. So Joel and I attacked the moguls, our passion making up for precision.

As I came to a stop on the edge of a drop-off halfway down the run, my left ski popped off. Because the hill was so steep, it continued for a bit before resting at the base of another drop-off. I removed the remaining ski, and as I started down to collect the other, Joel wiped out above me and lost his skis in the same spot. We climbed down together, both laughing at this point like little boys who had stolen their uncle's cigarettes. As I reattached my left ski, Joel handed me the other. Both of us were wearing rental skies so they looked identical. The only difference was that I'm a size 10 ½ while Joel is a size 12.

"See ya at the bottom," I said, as I stepped off the drop. I cleared the best of the moguls and then went into my Olympic form, putting my head down and squatting low. I "let the hill take me." And then, at nearly record speeds, my right ski simply disappeared. One moment I had two skis and the next I had one less. It just came off. What followed was a wipeout of such violent scope that I think for a moment even God held His breath. Halfway through the tumble, I felt my arm tear out of its socket, and a little farther along it popped back in. Finally, I came to a stop.

After a cautious examination of all my body parts to make sure nothing worse had happened, I turned my head to see my brother come to a stop right in front of me. He was laughing! "That was awesome, bro!" he said as if I had put on a show. And then, as an afterthought, "Are you all right?"

I lay there while we discussed my injury and the strange circumstance of my ski suddenly coming off. As he helped me up, he said, "It's odd your ski would just fall off, mine is really tight. I had a hard time getting it on after you left." I was too hurt to actually kill Joel right then and there, so I just talked about doing it.

Now, years later, my right arm doesn't work as good as my left, and when I try to start a lawn mower, I have to be careful. And maybe I'm not invincible, maybe. And I have noticed since the triple black, I ski a little differently too. If I start to get a little out of control, I experience this odd feeling—I think it's called fear. My mind starts shouting in a panicked tone "careful," and though I have heard it before, it's never been so demanding as these last few years.

When I was a younger man, I prayed some insane, radical prayers. They went something like this: "God, do what You need to do so You can use me for Your purposes. Purify me! I want Your fire! I want Your truth, Your justice. Make me hungry! Make me thirsty!" Then with the zeal of youth, I would step off the edge and dive headlong into the future. I would ski with reckless abandon, and sometimes I'd make it without wiping out, but it seems more times than not I would experience a wild ride ending in a violent and often painful tumble.

It happens. You know, falling down, making a mess of things. Sometimes it happens because someone else messed up. Sometimes it happens because you missed something. And then there are the times it seems to happen for no good reason at all. One moment you're flying high, a shoo-in for the next Winter Games, and the next moment one of your skis disappears and you find yourself triple-blacked at the bottom of the mountain with lungs full of snow.

I have chased my idea of God over so many mountainsides and have experienced more than one crash and burn. I have found myself broken at the bottom of many "mountains." Recently my prayers have transformed from the brash and desperate "even if I have to die with You, I will not forsake You," to the hope-filled whisper of "Lord, You know all things…."

Give a Man a Sword

Cover me, care for me, love me
Keep me Yours

I used to think Peter denied Christ simply out of fear for his own life. But I don't believe that anymore. When Jesus tells Peter he will deny Him three times, Peter flat-out refuses: *"Even if I have to die with You, I will not deny You"* (Matt. 26:35 NKJV). When we look at all the Gospels together, we get a good picture of that night in Gethsemane. And you know what? Peter told the truth, he did step up. He did step out, even to the point of giving his life. He pulled his sword out and swung it.

Peter didn't intend for his sword to miss, however. He wasn't just going for an ear, he was trying to take someone's head off. I think swinging the sword was as bold, if not bolder, than when Peter got out of the boat and walked on water. The second he swung the sword, he made a choice to be something other than a fisherman or even a disciple; he chose to be a murderer. He chose to be a criminal for Jesus.

Peter was good on his word to Jesus. "Even if I have to die with You"—that was the decision he made when he swung that sword. We all know Peter didn't understand, but I wonder, was he supposed to? In Luke's Gospel, just before they go to the garden, Jesus tells the disciples that "difficult times" are coming and they should go and get a sword (see Luke 22:36).

So what else was Peter to do but use the sword he'd been told to get? It's a fairly logical conclusion. If Jesus asked Peter to get a sword, it's not a large step to think he might be expected to use it. Yet when Peter stepped out, like he had many times before, and used the sword, when he gave his life on behalf of Jesus, he got it so wrong. Jesus rebuked him. What's more, Jesus heals the fella Peter de-eared. Then Peter, along with all the other disciples, having no idea what to do next, fled.

Can you imagine Peter's sorrow, his confused anguish? Still, his love for Christ draws him to follow behind, and when confronted with knowing Jesus, he denies Him—three times. And I wonder what was left for him to do? Peter's denial of Christ wasn't about fear of death, it was way worse—he was disillusioned with Life.

Peter was utterly lost. Everything he believed had just been destroyed. He was terrified, not of death, but of life without hope, of life without the Life Giver. It was disillusionment that caused Peter to deny Christ. In fact, I would go so far as to say Peter had fearlessly defended his Savior, his friend. He had followed wholeheartedly, even bringing and using the sword Jesus told him he would soon need.

And he got it completely wrong. He hadn't learned to dance yet…

A Penny in His Pocket

Come, let's go up to the mountain
Come, let's worship beneath the cross
Come, let's know our Savior's journey
And find our story in His song

I was listening to a song recently by Imogen Heap. The song lyrics are: "But then it's your life / but you've only got one." Years ago I told God I would be like a penny in His pocket and He could spend me any way He wanted. I've come to the realization that God has many pennies and spends them liberally on whatever pleases His heart. To me, at those battered and disillusioned times in my life, those moments of desperate disappointment, He has seemed to be the opposite of frugal, almost casually spending on whims.

The song lyrics suggest "it's my life," but it is not my life—it's His. I gave it to Him years ago and He took me at my word. Ever since, He has been spending me in ways I rarely understand, often causing disillusionment along the way. Just when I think I get it, I experience another failure, one more to add to the pile. I step out bold in my passion for Him and come back reeling from a fist to the jaw. It's like some kind of violent dance.

I have had great ideas in my life, godly, noble visions. My heavenly Father gave some of them to me and I've had my own to match. I've dragged God along with me on some of these ideas—these visions that were not completely surrendered. There is nothing more exhausting than trying to fit God into one of your plans.

I've also followed Him wholeheartedly and watched all my efforts fail. I've gotten ahead of God and I've trailed behind. I've fallen asleep in the garden and I've swung my sword. And I've wept on my face at the only place to fall, a hard place called the cross, a beautiful place called the cross.

The pathway God has led me on has at times seemed to be counter to His promises. And there have been seasons in my life where the only thing I can say to God is, "I don't understand, this doesn't look good, this doesn't feel good either." What's more, in those moments, it almost feels as if God doesn't seem really concerned with me being able to understand.

I believe I will be a part of what my Father is doing on the earth. It is my destiny. It is my promise since birth. I've been aware of it for years, and all that time my heavenly Father has been sometimes gently and sometimes violently grooming me. "Not my will but Your will be done," I've said to Him. And He's taken me seriously.

Remember the lawn mower and the triple black diamond? I still need to tell you about the ledge.

The Ledge

To die with Him, it is our journey
To live again and know His love

Mount Finlayson was a favorite climb that was close by—it was something we could do in a day. My dad, Joel, and I would start out on the marked trail and in good Clark fashion find an alternate route that was a little more challenging. On this particular day, we were quite a ways up and had climbed our way over to a series of steeply angled rock ledges when I slipped. I was on my back as I slid over the first ledge, about a four-foot drop. I was still a good way from the ultimate cliff edge, so I felt all was under control, but instead of stopping I continued sliding on my back, increasing in speed as I headed for the next drop-off. I scrambled for anything to grab onto but couldn't seem to slow myself down. As I slid over the second ledge, all I could see was sky, and I thought, "This is it," only to fall five feet onto another rock ledge and start sliding again. Once more I fought to stop the slide, but once more I was flung over the edge. Again I thought I was dead, but there was another ledge. This time I found a crevice in the rock and was able to finally stop my fall.

I remember lying there on that rock, my breath short, my heart raging. I started checking limbs—nothing was broken, just cuts, bruises, and torn fingernails. On trembling legs I stood and began to climb back to the guys. As I cleared the last ledge and looked up, my dad yelled, "You all right?"

"I think so," I panted out.

There was a short pause, and then he started laughing as his look of terror turned to relief. Then Joel started laughing too. It took me a moment to join in. By the time I had climbed back up to them, our laughter echoed halfway to heaven.

Looking back, one of the clearest parts of that memory is, from my falling vantage point, each drop-off was my last. I died three times that day only to find there was another ledge below to catch me. I tell this story because it has often seemed like my pursuit of God and His promise has been much the same—almost as if God has invited me to know Him through the experience of not just the climb but the helpless falls along the way as well.

A Matter of Trust

God was looking on me battered by the wind
To see if I would stumble, to see if I would bend...

Just before Jesus was betrayed and handed over to the Jewish religious leaders, He said to Peter, *"Simon, I've prayed for you in particular that you not give in or give out. When you have come through your time of testing, turn to your companions and give them a fresh start"* (Luke 12:31-32 MSG).

Peter gave the typical Peter headfirst response: "I will, even if the other disciples don't." Then Jesus, just after telling Peter He is praying for him to keep faith, says the craziest thing: *"Before the rooster crows today, you will deny three times that you know Me"* (Luke 22:34). Essentially Jesus is saying, "Hey, Pete, you will deny Me; you will fail Me."

It's hard for me to wrap my head around this. It seems cruel. It feels as though Jesus set Peter up to fail. He was already going to the cross. Wasn't it already painful and confusing enough for Peter? Wasn't the test big enough just to be a disciple of Jesus during this time? Why add to the trauma?

Years ago, while writing this, and with tears in my eyes, I asked my Father to please show me why this was necessary. And here is what I believe He gave me: Jesus wasn't looking for Peter to understand, and this had nothing to do with Peter passing a test; it was an invitation to discover his promise, to endure for the joy on the other side—resurrection life. He was learning to dance.

> "Never give a man a sword who can't dance."
>
> —CELTIC PROVERB

After Jesus had risen from the grave, He met with the disciples out on a beach. Jesus and Peter went for a walk, and then Jesus asked Peter the same question three times: "Do you love Me, Peter?" I think you could also phrase the question this way: "Peter, can I trust you with a sword?"

Peter's response? "Lord, You know all things. You know that I love You." It's a powerfully transformed response from the one given days earlier. There was no reckless ambition, no arrogant claims, no brash self-made man. He was surrendered and gentle and full of grace and mercy and infinitely trustworthier then the fella who had swung that sword.

Jesus says, "Feed My sheep." And with that commission, Peter was empowered to live his promise fully untamed. And with that commission, Jesus released an anointing on Peter any believer would want.

That day on the beach, Peter learned the sword Jesus had told them about was not an extension of his arm but rather of his heart— the power of his sword was not found in determination, or ambition, or his own strength, but in surrender. It meant trading his insecurities and fears for God's always-good love, trading his self-consciousness for God-consciousness, trading his idea of revolution for God's. When you're fully surrendered, when you can see the way He sees, you're free and empowered to forgive, serve, love, and dance.

The Peter from the garden couldn't be trusted to live untamed. He couldn't be trusted to swing a sword until he understood brokenness, until he had become intimate with surrender, until he had learned to dance. Jesus revealed it is not by might and not by power, but only by His Spirit. He was building the foundation of His church upon Peter's revelation of surrender and resurrection life.

Just days earlier, Peter believed absolutely in his love for Jesus. You couldn't have convinced him otherwise. He was willing to murder for Jesus. A man who doesn't know how to dance is a dangerous man, even if he's a disciple. He might just kill you. However, on the other side of disillusionment, on the other side of the cross, Peter was empowered to love Jesus not in brash boldness but with trust and humility. "Lord, You know that I love You." His ownership of the cross experience from denial to redemption, death to resurrection, was what empowered him to be life to his friends.

Before the cross Peter trusted in his love for Jesus. After the cross Peter trusted in Jesus's love for him. Faith is always about where your trust is placed. And that is where our promise lives, within the marriage of surrendered trust and untamed faith.

This painful testing that Peter experienced was an absolutely essential part of his story. It was never about Peter's understanding or success; it was about his faith. Jesus knew Peter would deny Him but He also knew Peter would finally be set free and empowered to discover the joy and fullness of his promise on the other side. This was Peter's redemption story—heart, soul, mind, and strength.

Amazingly, because of the cross, because of grace, we can fail Jesus and not be failures. In fact, to think otherwise belittles what He did at Calvary. Outside of His grace we are not capable of loving Jesus. Inside of His grace we are not capable of failing Him. We can get it wrong, but in believing get it right. We won't always under-stand the journey, and that's the point. We have to learn the dance steps of disillusionment where God shatters our illusions until our hearts are in full alignment with His. Then it's our joy to trust Jesus, and it's His joy to work it all to His glory and our good.

Our Father is faithful in His preparation of us when releasing His power and authority—when giving us a sword. The wilder we want to live for Him, the more intimate we must be with surrender. It's about trusting when we don't understand, about enduring in faith even when we have failed, and about learning to dance.

The Fire

I stood on the edge to see what I could see
Saw Your bride enraptured in the song of Your love
In the fires of Your glory

After a time of worship, Jeremy shared a vision he had. He saw a fire. One man walked up to it, then stepped around it, and continued walking. Another walked up to the fire, stepped in, and then quickly jumped out and continued on his way. He said the third man was me, and when I got to the fire, I jumped in and stayed.

I thought about this for a moment. I surely was in the fire at the time, and though it seemed I was the idiot in this scenario, I immediately realized the only reason I was in the fire was because Jesus was in the fire too. And what do you learn to do in the fire? Dance. And why does Jesus want me to learn to dance? He's got a sword for me to wield. It's part of my promise. And I believe it's part of yours too.

> *Pure gold put in the fire comes out of it proved pure; genuine faith put through this suffering comes out proved genuine. When Jesus wraps this all up, it's your faith, not your gold, that God will have on display as evidence of his victory* (1 Peter 1:7 MSG).

Chapter 10

Favor

Pharmaceuticals

I saw the stars tonight, You were there
I saw them burning bright, You were there

I'm not much of an academic sort. As a kid I attended our very own "church school," and in third grade I was held back. I found out late in my twenties this was not due to poor grades, as my parents had been told, but to the pastor's desire to see every grade represented evenly. This is understandable. "Symmetry is peace of mind," I always say. There were five third graders moving to fourth and one second grader moving to third, so my best friend Chris and I were held back.

I think this incident played a role in me not being much of the academic sort. It's not that I grew up thinking I was stupid, but it also never occurred to me I might be a genius. Who knows, if it hadn't happened, maybe I would have come up with an alternate source of energy or something. Maybe. Maybe I would have gone on after Bible college, put some letters behind my name, and made millions in pharmaceuticals. But I didn't, and that's why I just had to use spell check.

So instead of "smarts," I became intrigued by wisdom. These two things are not the same. Though *smart* can sometimes look like wisdom, they are not even remotely similar. In fact, they are often so far apart that if they were in the same room together, there would be a riot, except wisdom would never let that happen because he's too smart.

As a kid I was told Solomon was the wisest man outside of Jesus to walk the planet. There was one story in which Solomon displayed his wisdom that first offended and then amazed my young imagination. I still remember the night my dad read it to me from my very own picture Bible.

Two mothers were claiming one baby boy. They brought him to wise Solomon and each said, "He's *my* baby!" The first mother suggested the second had accidently suffocated her own boy while sleeping and then traded babies in the night. The second mother denied it.

Solomon simply said, "Give me my sword and the baby. I will cut him right down the middle. Then you can each have a half."

At this point in the story I interrupted my dad to let him know how disgusted and disappointed I was with Solomon. How on earth could he be considered "wise" when he was about to do something so horrific and stupid?

But then the first mother cried out, "Please, have mercy! Don't kill the baby. The second mother responded with a more calloused attitude "Seems fair to me."

Once Solomon and I heard both responses, we were able to discern which woman was the real mother. And I came into agreement with God's opinion of Solomon: "The fella was impressive!" I thought.

When I was a boy in my father's (David's) house, still tender, and an only child of my mother. Then he taught me, and he said, "Lay hold of my words with all your

heart; keep my commands, and you will live. Get wisdom,
get understanding..." (Proverbs 4:3-5).

In his own words, Solomon describes how his father David had taught him to pursue wisdom—to hunger for it.

The first time my dad read the story of Solomon and the baby, a hunger was birthed in my heart. I wanted wisdom, like Solomon had. There were several years throughout my childhood and teens where I asked God daily and specifically for wisdom. Like Solomon, wisdom became a pursuit.

Get What You Want and Need

Every mystery unveiled
Every secret revealed
You were there

After David died and Solomon is handed the reins to an established and thriving kingdom, he must have felt an incredible weight of responsibility, and he was probably a little overwhelmed. Then God came to him in a dream and said, "Because of your father, I am going to offer you whatever you want—fame, fortunes—just name it and it's yours" (see 1 Kings 3:10-15).

As a kid I imagined this God encounter was kind of like having a genie offer you one wish, except God is real and I was pretty sure genies weren't. Either way, I knew what I would have said: "I'll have one hundred more wishes, please." I remember thinking I was smart for coming up with that, then I remembered being held back and realized I probably just got lucky.

Solomon says, "I don't want wealth or health or death to my enemies. What I want—what I need—is wisdom." God's response was revealing: "Because you asked for wisdom, I will give you all the other things as well."

In my youth God used this story to impress upon me that wisdom was actually something you could choose. I understood that wisdom far exceeded "smart." It was clear God wasn't impressed by intellect but by a man who was pursuing wisdom. Since then, I've come to an understanding that wisdom is another way to describe God. Wisdom reveals God's thoughts and presence.

Solomon surrendered all the other options for God's thoughts and presence, in a word, revelation. Solomon meets Wisdom face to face and realizes all his questions and all his needs are answered there. Wisdom is a revelation of the nature of God, it's truth revealed.

What's amazing is that wisdom is always connected to favor. You can't receive wisdom or *revelation* without experiencing favor. Favor follows wisdom like Christmas follows Christmas Eve or *Rocky VI* follows *Rocky V.*

"Won't This Be Fun?"

Till Your bride knows Your glory
Till it burns in our soul

How would a fisherman describe favor, is favor discovered in the act of fishing or is favor defined by the catch? Yeah I know, this is *the* timeworn, thought-provoking, and paradigm-shifting question. Stick with me though, I think we may finally have some answers.

Recently I was introduced to a new experience—the overnight family camping trip. You know, a tent, air mattresses, fold-out seats, a fire in a pit with wood provided to you by the state park, and, of course, restrooms with running water. Having spent my teen years in the wild Northwest, I had a more rugged and what I believed correct camping experience.

Before leaving, whenever Karen referenced our weekend as a camping trip, I would correct her. "We are not going camping, darlin',"' I would say. I like to imagine I sounded a bit like Hannibal from the A-Team: "True camping is a roll of toilet paper, some mixed nuts, a jackknife, duct tape, a Band-Aid, and three days from civilization. What we are about to do, my dear, is essentially a half step beyond sleeping in a backyard tent." I admit, I was a little obnoxious.

We had so much fun! We sat around a fire and made s'mores and drank coffee and hot chocolate. And because Karen is a culinary genius we ate like royalty. No mixed nuts; I'm talking steak and foil potatoes for dinner, bacon and eggs for breakfast. We slept in a tent, all five of us in our PJs, and sleeping bags, on air mattresses, with lots of pillows, and an extra king size comforter just in case it got too cold. We wrestled and told stories and giggled. All and all, *family* camping is a different but no less enjoyable experience.

I called my dad when we got home and told him about our new adventure. I also let him know how I passed a sorta-tradition on to my kids that he had sorta passed on to me when I was a kid: fishing.

My dad is not a fisherman, or maybe he is a fisherman without fish-catching favor? Either way, every couple of years he would somehow get the idea that fishing could be fun. So off we would go with a bucket of worms or whatever bait he had been told the mackerel, trout, salmon etc. were biting. He would hype my siblings and me up with phrases like "catching the big one" and "this will be so fun." And in our formative years we would buy in. But it was always the same; our early morning anticipation became late morning disappointment and early afternoon disgust as the better part of a day was spent untangling line with almost always the same results: sunburns and no fish.

By the time I was twelve I strongly disliked fishing. I could think of a million better ways to spend a day—Mrs. Pac-Man, Choose Your Own Adventure, even reruns of *Little House on the Prairie* rated higher. However, on our recent family camping trip, I found myself echoing my dad's "catching the big one," and "this will be so fun" phrases to my little ones as we walked from our campsite to the lake with our $12 Wal-Mart fishing poles and our bucket of worms.

It was just like I remember—lots of untangling, sunburns, and no fish.

My dad laughed as I assured him that our sorta fishing tradition hadn't ended with him. I too was developing an early and potentially strong dislike of fishing in my children.

However, something tells me fishing could be so fun, possibly even exciting, if we would just catch something.

> [Jesus] *called out to them, "Friends, haven't you any fish?" "No," they answered. He said, "Throw your net on the right side of the boat and you will find some." When they did, they were unable to haul the net in because of the large number of fish* (John 21:5-6).

The disciples appeared to have fished all night and caught nothing. I think we have all experienced that. Long days, and nights, and weeks, and years of fishing without the wonder of the catch.

And then with a word from Jesus, the disciples, using the same nets and the same technique, cast their nets in again, and then there is a suddenly moment—lots of fish. More than they could handle. This time it worked.

For me, this story raises thought-provoking and paradigm-shifting questions. You know, "What defines favor?"

Favor is a word I have often been confused by. To me favor has implications. It suggests results, breakthrough, and for the fisherman, fish, lots and lots of them. But I've spent a great portion of my life "fishing" without experiencing much "catching." I have become proficient at mending and casting nets and sailing. But to be honest, there have been times when, due to the lack of fish, I have even questioned whether I was really a fisherman or just a stubborn dude with vintage gear and an old boat.

I think it's amazing that David taught his son Solomon to seek wisdom. David prepared Solomon's heart to ask God for the very thing God desired to give him. I would like to suggest that David's instruction birthed Solomon's hunger and Solomon's hunger was the invitation to God meeting him and offering him such amazing choices. God (Wisdom) was drawn to Solomon's heart to know wisdom. Kind of like the instruction by Jesus to have the disciples throw their nets on the other side of the boat was drawn by the disciples' act of fishing.

My point, if the disciples had been sleeping instead of fishing, Jesus would have never been able to release fish-catching favor.

I am learning that favor is released when we are faithful with our hunger. I think favor looks like days, weeks, months, and years of fishing without catching until we are in the right place with the right vintage gear, and the right experience, and the right knowledge to hear the right words, "throw your net on the other side." And voila, fish, lots and lots of them.

The disciples were positioned to catch fish on the morning of Jesus's instructions. And that's huge. In fact, I think that's half of what favor looks like—fishing without the catching.

The favor to catch fish can only be released to the person that is already fishing. And it's a journey of faith. Favor is a process. As we choose wisdom, we grow in wisdom and therefore favor until *suddenly* we are fisherman who catch fish. I think favor is as much about fishing as it is about catching.

So in answer to the question asked at the beginning of this section—what does favor look like to a fisherman?—well, ultimately it looks like catching fish, lots and lots of fish. But before that, it looks like lots and lots of fishing without the catching.

I am learning that favor is neither in the title nor in the catch. Favor is in His promise. Favor is discovered in His voice. I believe that every promise from God—yours and mine—comes with the favor of God to see it fully realized. And the fishing without catching is how we discover it.

As I wrote earlier, the promises of God are not guarantees; they are invitations. To fully embrace these invitations, we must grow in both wisdom and favor; we must live for our *future* promise in the *present*. By faith, we position ourselves in lack so we are ready for plenty. We are invited to live for breakthrough until we are living from breakthrough. Favor looks like days, months, and even years faithfully fishing until one day we *suddenly* catch fish.

Now let's look at it from another angle…but don't worry, I'll get back to the fish.

Fifteen Years Old, Unmarried and Pregnant

I hope I attain something that sustains
Something beautiful

Sometimes it's easy to confuse the favor of man with the favor of God, almost like two mothers wrestling over the same baby. I'm not as wise as Solomon, but I'm going to try to cut to the truth.

Years ago I heard a teaching by a missionary named Heidi Baker about favor that shed light on my own journey. We all know the central story of Mary and Joseph and the birth of Jesus. But there is so much depth there, especially in light of what God's favor looks like. It is a depth both terrifying and beautiful.

The angel Gabriel comes to Mary in her room and says, *"Greetings, you who are highly favored! The Lord is with you"* (Luke 1:28). And then he quickly follows it up with, *"Do not be afraid, Mary, you have found favor with God"* (Luke 1:30). Then Gabriel goes on to tell Mary she is going to give birth to Jesus. It will be a virgin birth, and He will be the Son of God. This section of the story reveals the favor of God in a way that is at odds with how most of us would define it.

Think about this for a moment. As soon as the angel leaves, Mary—who is estimated to have been fourteen or fifteen years old at the time—has to go into the next room and explain to her parents what the favor of God looks like. Can you imagine what this would look like?

"Mom, Dad, I just had an encounter with an angel and he said not to be afraid and that I am favored of God!"

Mom and Dad are smiling ear to ear. Mom, almost giddy, says, "That's wonderful news dear! It so amaz—"

Mary cuts her off. "Mom! There's more!" She takes a shaky breath. "I know I'm young, I know I'm not yet married, but Mom, Dad...did I mention the angel said I am favored? I did? Yeah, well... ha, I'm pregnant!"

Fifteen years old, unmarried and pregnant in a culture that stones you for that sorta thing. That's what favor first looked like for Mary.

Do you realize the favor of God on this girl forced her to live with the stigma of promiscuity? Mary was given one of the most astounding promises ever. She was honored above every other woman on the face of the planet. She is the earthly mother of the God who created everything. She is the woman who bore Love in human form, humanity's redemption in the flesh. And this favor made its entrance, at least to the eyes of man, in the form of shame.

The moment God reveals His promise, the moment we get a glimpse into our future, God releases His favor and it often looks something like Mary's did. Favor doesn't mean an easy life; rather, it is the evidence of His pleasure and trust. Favor reveals our identity and our promise. It says, "You are *going to be* a mom to the Savior of the world."

God's favor may shock us at first. It may look nothing like what we had thought before, it may overwhelm, and it may even cause us to feel helpless and powerless. Think about it in terms of Mary. Favor looked like Jesus, the Promised One, in her womb for nine months before He was born. Favor felt like nine months of growing and morning sickness and blue jeans that didn't fit anymore—all that pregnancy stuff. Favor also destroyed Mary's reputation. It opened her to ridicule and broken relationships and heartache. In a word, it was *hard*. But in two words, it was *God's favor.*

I have asked God for favor most of my life. I have also had moments where my Father let me know He was well pleased and that He loved and trusted me. I've also had moments of revelation regarding my identity and promise. And then I would wonder why life was so hard, why we were in such discomfort, why there were seasons of such loneliness, why such disregard from the church? It got so hard at times I questioned whether I was favored or cursed. But when I heard this message on favor from Heidi Baker, I realized I've had His astounding favor all along, it's just been the fifteen-year-old, unmarried, pregnant favor of God.

Favor of God, Favor of Man

Man was made for wonder
And trust was made by God

> *And Jesus grew in wisdom and stature, and in favor with*
> *God and men* (Luke 2:52).

God releases His favor and then invitees us to believe. And believing is how we steward His favor to maturity.

We believe even when they say, "You're too young, you need more discipleship," or, "You're too old, your time has come and gone." We believe when we are ridiculed for what appears to be failure. We believe while in the wilderness or at the cross, we believe while facing the giants, and we believe when those around us have lost heart and turned away. We believe when it's not cool to believe, when it looks irrelevant or foolish or improper or radical or risky. We believe when we feel horrible and our clothes no longer fit and we just can't get comfortable.

Like Mary, we believe and in so doing we learn how to carry our promise to full term even under intense criticism from those around us, including our peers. We learn how to believe in the midst of fifteen-year-old, unmarried, pregnant favor. And we do this because we know the promise is always yes and amen, but sometimes it's also *not yet.*

I am convinced that when the favor of God comes to maturity, God releases the favor of man upon us as well. When the favor of man is partnered with the favor of God, His Kingdom is exponentially expanded through our promise. It's called a *suddenly moment.* In other words, suddenly there are fish—lots and lots of them. Told you I'd get back to the fish.

This is called a legacy, and it's why we are here, it's why we have the promise—to see His Kingdom come on earth as it is in heaven. In the disciples' fishing story, the fish represent abundance and breakthrough, the fullness of favor. Our promise is not only for us but for those around us. You can only give what you have—the more fish you have, the more you can give. Our promise is meant to become our legacy, and our legacy is always about giving the way Jesus gave—powerfully, miraculously, from heaven.

There are so many stories in the Bible that reveal this. For instance, Joseph, the son of Isaac, is given his promise in two dreams. With the promise, God releases His favor and then Joseph experiences the maturing process, gestation—years and years in slavery, serving in obscurity, hidden, learning, growing, becoming, staying the course. Joseph continued to believe God, and when the favor of man was released through Pharaoh, there was a suddenly moment, and Joseph went big time. He essentially became the leader of the known world and he gave with power and authority—his favor saved a nation from starvation.

Then there is David. He is given his promise, and with it the favor of God is released. And David's favor? It looked like years of dodging spears and then running from a mad king intent on killing him; it looked like restraint and honoring those without honor. Then there was a suddenly moment, David became king and his favor led a nation into its greatest and most peaceful era ever. But not until it was time.

One more thought here. It's important for us to understand that God must be the One to release us into the favor of man. We should not take it for ourselves. Both Joseph and David could have taken the favor of man before God released it—Joseph when his first master's wife tempted him, and David with his opportunities to kill Saul with his own hands. However, both men waited for God's suddenly moment.

Along the way, we will have opportunities to gain the favor of man, but these will be in direct conflict with Wisdom. Wisdom will guide us into honor, trust, long-suffering, and love. But there will be a moment when the favor of God partners with the God-released favor of man, and in that moment we will get to see a *suddenly*.

Suddenlys are holy moments—where we once appeared irrelevant, suddenly we are defining relevant; where once we were running for our lives, suddenly we are stepping into a position of authority; suddenly we are seeing the promise in all its wonderful glory; suddenly the Kingdom is exponentially advanced.

Typically, the bigger the suddenly moment, the more years of backstory. Suddenlys always come on the heels of waiting, of patient trust and radical believing. They come after we have spent the night fishing and haven't caught a thing, and they are accompanied by Wisdom's voice calling out across the water, "Throw your net on the other side." And suddenly there are fish. Lots and lots of them!

I want to catch fish. I imagine you do as well. I want all of God's favor. I live in the sweet anticipation of Jesus walking up on the beach and saying, "Hey, no fish? Throw your nets out on the other side. Now is the suddenly moment, now I'm going to fill them. Now is the time to participate in miracles. Now is the time to engage."

You know, Jesus walked the planet for thirty-three years, and as far as we know there were no miracles in the first thirty. But suddenly...

Favor is discovered when we put our trust in God's love, when the promise of God is believed and faithfully acted on. He speaks, we hear, we trust, we obey, we risk, and *suddenly* fish—lots and lots of them.

I Am

No blind eye nor deaf ear
No more wondering if You are here

One of the names of God is "I Am," which means, He is the God of right now. Yesterday He was God and tomorrow He will still be God, but I really want to know Him as I Am—the God of right now. If I know Him as I Am, then right now I have access to Wisdom, His presence, and revelation.

Solomon's life promised and Jesus's LIFE revealed that every question humanity is asking is answered in a greater revelation of God's presence. I want His presence. I want to dream His dreams. I want my joy found in His presence, my peace found in His will, my freedom found in surrender, and my surrender the birthplace of an untamed existence.

If I know Him as I Am, then I will have access to Him in any and every way I need Him—His love, His grace, His glory, His power. These and other revelations are what I must experience in order to keep on believing, especially during those long "fifteen-year-old, unmarried, pregnant favor" of God seasons. I can trust when I ask,

"Uh, Father, about this favor You have given me…are You still here?" He will respond, "Yes. I Am."

True Wild Blaze

So we go walking out in this field
To claim our destiny

When Maddy was born, we prayed over her name. We loved Madeleine for a first name, and when Karen suggested "True" for her middle name, we both just knew it was perfect. She really is True. When Ethan came, we chose Wilde for a middle name. At that point we began to realize God was choreographing our kids' middle names with what He was working in us. You see, if we live true, we can live wild. If we live surrendered, we can live untamed. But surrendered and untamed weren't really middle name choices. I'm just sayin'.

So when Eva, our third child, was on her way, we really felt like God was going to give us another part of the revelation. Just before she was born, God gave Karen the name Blaze, and now we have a beautiful little Eva Blaze. What's amazing is when a believer begins to live within the partnership of true and wild, they get to set the world ablaze. When we live surrendered and untamed, we engage our promise. God releases His favor on our lives, and we get to blaze for Him.

This middle name stuff really is cool. It's all tied to conception and gestation and birth and life and favor and promise…and a good, loving God. I feel I have the smallest grasp of these truths, like a newborn hanging onto the Father's fingers. But I'll tell you this: I'm hanging on for dear life—the dearest life there is, one hidden in the very hand of God. There are stories of men and women throughout history who set the world ablaze with the goodness of God. I want my story to be one of those stories. And I desire the same for Karen and Maddy True and Ethan Wilde and Eva Blaze. As for me and my house, we want Wisdom and favor and fish—lots of them. We will trust, and in the fullness of time…

Jason: You're listening, right, God, as I type this?

God: I Am.

Chapter 11

Dreaming like an Old Man

The A-Team

A rift at dawn and stormy hearts
Another song a brand-new start

I've been told I have the wisdom and leadership skills of Hannibal, the brute strength and loyalty of B.A., the crazy humor and daring of Murdock, the imaginative resourcefulness and suave deliciousness of Face Man…and Amy's eyes. Who told me that? Whatever.

In my late teens and early twenties, I thought I knew how to dream. It looked a lot like a good A-Team episode. I'd travel to a new place, encounter a beautiful woman who thought I was—what shall we say?—delicious. I would discover an injustice being perpetrated by a Bad Dude. I would then go to his place of business, a rundown western bar, I'd walk in, all cocky and clever, look him straight in the eye and say in a mocking southern accent, "It smells like ignorant wretch in here."

Bad Dude: (incredulous) This don't involve you, stranger. Get lost.

187

Jason: (calmly sarcastic) I don't think we're gonna be friends. I'll give you till noon tomorrow to clear outta town.

Bad Dude: (furious) Get 'em boys!

Then one of his thugs took a swing at me. With ease, I slid away, and using his momentum against him, I helped him out the plate-glass window. Just then B.A. showed up and in good "bad attitude" fashion, knocked a few heads together. Face Man, who had been sitting at the bar, rolled his eyes and proceeded to walk to the exit while trying not to spill the contents of his drink—alas, some poor fella bumped into him and Face was compelled to get involved.

Soon we had a real ruckus on our hands. Just when we thought we'd gained the upper hand, the Bad Dude replaced fists with guns. We were forced to dive for cover. That's when Murdock pulled up in the van. With bullets flying but never landing, we made our way to the van and then had to wait for Murdock to get out and let B.A. drive.

Yeah, I dreamed in the language of an '80s action TV series.

Life was going to be an exciting and sometimes dangerous adventure. And if I got shot along the way, I imagined it would be a mere flesh wound, not the Monty Python kind of "mere." And if I got captured, Bad Dude would probably hold me in an auto mechanic shop, or something like that. That's where I would build a vehicle out of duct tape (thanks, MacGyver) and exhaust pipes. I would burst through the garage doors and run all the Bad Dude's cars off the road. I would put to right the wrongs.

Then I would kiss the girl, say something cool about plans coming together, exhale cigar smoke, and drive off into the sunset. Yes, my vision of the future was epic and could be wrapped up in a pretty bow in about forty-three minutes without commercials.

As a younger man, dreaming seemed as easy as breathing. But I'm getting older now. Over the last twenty years or so I've had some rude awakenings. Yes, I've traveled to new places and yes I've confronted the Bad Dude. But that's pretty much where the similarities to an episode of the A-Team end. You see, the bullets were real and they didn't miss. And they were Monty Python's interpretation of *mere* flesh wounds.

I've also spent countless years stuck in one mechanic shop after another. And when I finally escaped in my makeshift duct tape automobile, it got run off the road and then flipped several times. In my particular story I did get the beautiful girl, but I've had to apologize to her many times because she's been in the car with me.

I'm not as young as I once was. I've got the scars to prove it. I'm beginning to understand true dreaming isn't for the faint of heart, it isn't entered into lightly; rather, it's a radical act of faith. True dreaming isn't a PG TV show—it's gritty, it costs something, everything. Why? Because true dreaming is what you do after the car has flipped, after the bullets tore through flesh, after you have given your all and failed. I am learning that true dreaming is an old man's game.

A Greater Tomorrow Faith

So sweet to trust in Jesus and to take Him at His Word
And rest upon His promise, Oh for grace to trust Him more

In chapter 8 I told a story about how God brought our family through a journey in which we experienced financial hardship. He invited us to step directly in front of our Goliath and sling the sling. Karen and I learned how to trust in that season and we experienced breakthrough. We killed the giant.

Since that breakthrough, however, we have faced other financial hardships—even bigger giants. Our defeat of the first didn't mean we wouldn't face others down the road. But it did mean we could live surer in our trust and more powerful in our believing. The faith that is engaged today makes a greater faith available for tomorrow.

The Great Recession

In 2008, midway through the fourth year of running a thriving company, the economy hiccupped, which has now been dubbed "the Great Recession." I was part owner and wholly invested in a construction-based Internet company. Eighty percent of our sales were for new home construction, and this little economic meltdown seemed specifically targeted at, well, new home construction.

In one month our sales numbers were cut in half. The phone practically stopped ringing. At first, we hoped the recession was just a small blip on the radar. So we soldiered on. Money flew out of our bank account at an alarming rate. After our third month, we began to face the inevitable—it was time to make drastic cuts.

But it was too late. Within six months of the recession, the company God had miraculously led us into, the company that was once going to take care of my kids' college and give Karen and I financial freedom, was financially upside down. Within two years of the Great Recession I lost the company and was behind on my mortgage and nearly every other bill. Another vision mangled on the roadside, another failure by a son of God who was learning he wasn't a failure.

Vision and Dreams

Cause I've been dreaming for a time
A glorious climb, I must confess

> *In the last days, God says, I will pour out My Spirit on all people. Your sons and daughters will prophesy, your young men will see visions, your old men will dream dreams* (Acts 2:17).

It's only been in the last ten years that I have begun to quote that verse correctly. In my twenties I always got it backward. It made more sense that young men would dream dreams and old men would see visions. I'm not saying I am old now, but I am definitely getting older. I've come to understand that there is a difference between dreams and visions.

Vision is defined as "the act or power of anticipating that which will or may come to be." At eighteen, and over the following twenty or so years, I tested every projection, prodding and discovering both my Father's heart and mine. I was *anticipating* all the possible futures, and, in so doing, I was learning both who my Father was and my identity as His son. I was discovering the Promise Giver and my promise. When I was younger, every exciting possibility that popped into my head would have been categorized as a dream and often a God dream. But in hindsight, most of those dreams would be better defined as "your young men will see visions."

I think the difference between visions and dreams is this: dreams are hidden in our Father's heart and visions are how we discover them. Dreams are way bigger and more powerful than any words could ever express. They are the promises of God discovered through a revelation of the Promise Giver.

Old men dream dreams that are above and beyond imagination, and yet we've been invited to take the journey, to imagine, to envision, to search them out. And it's a scary and all-consuming journey, a journey that deepens trust, a journey for the faithful, a journey of discovering and believing He loves us, a journey into the fullness of our promise, an untamed life. It's a journey of vision and failure, vision and failure, vision and failure. It's also a journey where young men become old. And it's a good journey, because dreaming is an old man's game.

Before I go further, let me make this clear. Old men, in the context of this chapter, is not an age, it is a definition of the faith walk through failure, hard times and disappointment.

Old men have the most scars—they have the hardest memories, of war and death. It is old men who carry the pain of loss and brokenness. They have given their life to the King and His cause time and again. They have waited, and when they couldn't wait any more, they've waited some more.

Old men have done all they could to stand, and when they couldn't stand any longer, they still stood. They have died, been reborn, and died again. They have failed, and when they didn't think they could fail worse, they did. Old men have lost everything, and have done so more than once. It is the old men who have chased visions through the valley of the shadow of death and learned to trust, to rest, fearing no evil. And old men have chased vision into the heart of the Father's perfect love until both hearts beat in rhythm, until their every heartbeat can be trusted.

And then, with the full understanding of what dreaming costs, old men…well, they dream dreams. And the power and authority of their dreams pull heaven to earth in ways never before seen. Their dreams are the keys that "unlock any and every door." Their dreams are the yes on earth that resonates with the yes in heaven. Their dreams empower generations to live heaven on earth just as Jesus lived and promised.

And isn't that the promise He's given us all, that we could dream life-transforming, world-changing, saints-empowering, old-men dreams? I'm not saying I'm old, but by the goodness and grace of God, I'm getting older.

The Door Company

Jeremy and I had partnered with my dad and another fella to start an online door company. We sold high-end entryways, mostly residential, and mostly new construction. We offered custom-built wood or wrought iron doors—each one a beautiful work of art. Our typical customers were between the ages of forty and sixty. They were fairly wealthy—they had to be because our doors were fairly expensive.

One of my favorite sales was for a big-game hunter. He called one day and wanted to replace his entire entryway because he had just returned from a successful African safari where he'd killed a rhino. It had been stuffed and was being shipped stateside. He wanted it to be displayed in his front foyer, the obvious place for a stuffed rhino.

But he had a problem. His current front door entry was only large enough to accommodate the size of a stuffed cow. That's where we came in. We specialized in grand entries. For the right price, we could build him the rhino model.

I hope you don't sense any sarcasm while reading about what became known as "the rhino job." There really isn't any sarcasm involved at all. I have a stuffed monkey hanging from the chandelier in my entryway. Actually, that's a lie—I don't have a chandelier. Okay, maybe there's a little sarcasm.

I loved our door company. I loved selling doors to all kinds of people, from hunters who wanted to display their trophies to "mother earth" lovers who were committed to green products in the house they were building out of straw—seriously, straw. Cue the big bad wolf joke—obviously that ended up known as the "blow your house down" job.

The door company was a beautiful gift from my heavenly Father. In truth, I had never dreamed of owning a door company. Not once. Nor would I have ever thought it would be a part of my story, my promise. But I had already surrendered my promise back to my Father. This was His company, and I was fully committed to trusting Him. I thoroughly enjoyed running the company and Karen and I grew in wisdom and favor—we were thankful and blessed.

Over the first several years we experienced incredible favor with God and man. The business thrived. We grew in faithfulness and in stewardship, both practically and spiritually. We also got to eat steak along the way. I'm not saying we flew first class, just that we could afford steak every now and then.

Within the door industry we were celebrated. We were one of the first sellers to open up the online market, so we were the cool online guys. Our vendors liked us and our customers were many, and they were happy. It was a sweet time; we were living in the center of God's will.

When the Great Recession hit in 2008, Karen and I began a new journey into a greater faith, a deeper trust. And I began to discover even more of my promise. And it was about learning how to truly dream—like an old man.

Principles, Power, and Authority

I remember when I was fifteen needing a sum of money for a mission trip and feeling financially strained. I prayed with sincere faith Philippians 4:19: *"My God shall supply all of* (my) *needs according to His riches in glory by Christ Jesus"* (NKJV). The Scripture is true—God is our provider. And I chose to trust Him with all my finances that day. It was faith, it was right and good, and I was living at home with my parents.

In my mid-thirties, nearly two years after I lost the door company, the mortgage hadn't been paid in months and there was very little food in the pantry or fridge. I prayed the same prayer I had prayed when I was fifteen. "My God shall supply all my needs according to His glory—His goodness, and according to His nature—His perfect love." The Scripture was no truer than when I'd prayed it at fifteen, but the power behind my prayer was exponentially greater. This was because my circumstances had introduced me to a greater trust and more powerful revelation.

Reckless Abandon

Till I find my joy complete, let me see
Oh Love be my sweet witness

I was out for a run when my Father spoke to my heart. "Jason, I want you to dream with the expectation of a child." This invitation was just like God. It came on a day when I woke up to a phone call from a bill collector, followed by a call from a lawyer, followed by a call from another bill collector. This invitation came on a day when we had less then $5.00 to our names, including the change in the sofa. This invitation also came with a memory.

God brought back to my memory a day nearly twenty years earlier when Eric and I drove to the recording studio to track guitar and vocals for our nearly completed first full-length album. We mock interviewed each other for the *Rolling Stone* article we were certain was just around the corner.

Eric is my best friend and my brother-in-law. He is one of the most faithful and kind men I know. If you ever want to experience the goodness of God, just have a conversation with Eric. He was also the drummer of Fringe and may just be the best drummer on the planet.

"How does it feel to record the best album in a decade?" Eric asked in his best interviewer voice. "A decade?" I responded sarcastically, and we both laughed. Then I asked my question: "What's it feel like to be in a band with a singer-songwriter savant?" I asked. It felt like a valid question.

As I ran I found myself smiling at the sweet naive memory of when I was younger. Then my Father continued to speak to my heart: "I want you to dream with the reckless abandon you felt that day in the car with Eric."

It was an uncomfortable thought. We never interviewed for *Rolling Stone*—I have the scars to prove it. I had long since laid aside the visions of my younger self. I had given everything back to Him: music, my ideas of ministry, community, and, of course, most recently, the company. I'd been shot repeatedly; I had failed time and again. The idea of dreaming with a reckless abandon scared me.

Believe like a Child, Dream like an Old Man

As a sacred sky descends
Hey friends, it's time we got going

The day my Father asked me to dream with reckless abandon, He was inviting me to live in the tension of a faith that believes like a child and dreams in the power of an old man. Faith isn't blind to circumstances; faith believes regardless of the circumstances.

We have been invited to believe in the absolute expectation of a child and dream in the transformative power of an old man. It's called faith. It's a tension that leads to powerful transformation. The tension of this faith is where our promises are engaged and the whole world has access to it.

The old-man dream is in the young-man vision. Or as my hero-friend Bill Johnson says, "The oak is in the acorn." In every failed vision there is an opportunity to trust. This trust refines our hearts, we grow more sure, our faith becomes more powerful, more substantive, and more transformative, and then we dream old-men dreams.

Though I will always be young, I am getting older. I desire to believe like a child and dream like an old man. So when I pray, "God shall supply all my needs according to His riches and glory," I am not just praying from a principle but with power and authority.

I desire to believe like a child and dream old-man dreams that create both an atmosphere and opportunity for others' promises to encounter the Promise Giver. I desire to believe like a child and dream old-man dreams so cultures are transformed and those around me have access to the transformative power of His goodness.

Dreaming like an Old Man

I've been Your echo, I've been Your shadow
But my heart is to know You so I can be Your voice

Old-men dreams are available to sons and daughters who have chased down vision, failed, lived through the real pain of failure, and still believe with the reckless faith of a child in the absolute goodness of God's love. Old-men dreams are not about age; they are gifted through the journey into revelation. They are not a pretty concept or a good principle; neither are they the brash leap or the optimistic bent. Old-men dreams are a faith that has been tried through the fires of failure and even death.

It's the faith Peter experienced when he used a sword to advance a Kingdom that could only be advanced by Jesus becoming the sheath. Did Peter fail? Yes. But just because he failed doesn't mean he was a failure. The story doesn't end with death—it's never about failure or death. The story is always about resurrection, redemption, and revelation. Old-men dreamers are those who have joined Jesus, the Promise Giver, in that journey, the one where death isn't the point, but it's the only way to fully live.

When it was all said and done, Peter knew the good love of God in a way that wasn't dependent on him. This is the only Love with the power to redeem; this is Love with the authority to move mountains. This is the Love that empowered Peter to transform the world, the Love that became the foundation, a rock upon which the church would be built and the gates of hell would not prevail. This is the Love that possessed the keys of heaven to open any and every door, a love with the authority to say yes or no on earth and hear the echo in heaven. This powerful revelation of love was the promise Jesus gave Peter from the very beginning.

A true dream, one that is birthed in the heart of old-men dreamers, carries with it power and authority. Only a person who has experienced the death of vision, who has nailed vision to the cross, has access to the power of resurrection. When he dreams again, he dreams the dreams of heaven. And a dream that's birthed in heaven has power to transform the earth—it can change a family, a neighborhood, a city, and a nation. It grows exponentially and has eternal significance.

I believe true dreams are revelation of, and then partnership with, the Father's heart. You see, dreams are not meant to be possibilities; that's the role of vision. Dreams are meant to be prophetic declarations that create the future—they have authority and power to pull heaven to earth.

Here is another way to look at it: vision is about discovering our Father's nature. Dreaming happens as we see ourselves from His perspective. When we see ourselves through our Father's eyes, we are empowered to dream in the authority of our identity, our promise. Old-men dreams are birthed from our true identity, our promise. When we dream from who we truly are, we come into agreement with our heavenly Father, and step into the power and authority to see the dream realized. That's why dreaming like an old man is the most powerful thing we could ever do. It's the partnership with His heart and ours that pulls heaven to earth.

Of this I'm convinced: God wants us to dream with reckless abandon. Wide-open places, that's the heart of our Father for us. Jesus said we would do "greater works;" Jesus's life on earth, the high watermark for a miraculous life, is meant to be surpassed.

I believe greater works are available to old-men dreamers who are willing to dream untamed in the places of past failure, and their dreams carry the power of resurrection life. I am learning to not be offended by failure, to not be ashamed by weakness or insecure by lack. Instead, as I choose childlike surrender, as I express my faith in His love, I discover the Promise Giver in new ways, and I am invited to live untamed within my promise.

My prayer is that my heart would beat in sync with His so my words release heaven and my life yields love. My prayer is that my vision reveals His and my dreams transform the world around me, until the kingdoms of this world become the Kingdoms of our God.

As I lean into my forties, I have great expectation that when I pray, "God shall supply all my needs according to His riches and glory," my life will carry the authority of that prayer. The truth won't change, but my giving sure will. It will have all the power and authority of old-men dreams. When we believe as a child and dream like an old man, mountains are moved, Bad Dudes are destroyed, and generations are set free. I will always be young, but I thank God I am getting older.

Chapter 12

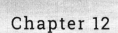

Calling All Bravehearts

Eggos and Juice Boxes

I turn my face to a blazing sun
Your glory falls, Your Kingdom comes

Recently, while Ethan was eating breakfast and over a mouthful of waffles, he informed me in a serious tone that he didn't want to have kids when he grew up. I could tell my seven-year-old had given it some deep thought.

"No kids? But you love kids," I said.

"Yes, I do, but I don't want any." He seemed sure.

"Why?" I asked.

"I don't want to have to share my Eggos," he said matter-of-factly. Then he paused, thought further, and then said, "Or my juice boxes."

"I hear you, man," I said commiserating. "Your mom makes me share too!" He nodded his agreement.

Later I told Karen about Ethan's deliberations and we had a good laugh. And we can laugh, for we know our son and he is a giver. Sometimes he needs to be reminded of this fact, but I have watched him and my girls live generously, and they have learned living generously from the same place I have—their bravehearted mother.

Karen is the most giving person I know. She truly amazes me on a daily basis. She spends time just thinking about what she can do that will bless the kids, myself, our family, friends, and even strangers. When she meets people, she starts dreaming of ways to bless them. When I asked her years ago how she knows what everyone wants for their birthdays, she said, "It's easy, babe. I listen when they tell me." It's not that people give her a verbal wish list for what they want. What she was saying is that she listens with a generous heart. When people talk, she hears what stirs them, and because she has positioned her heart to give, she is able to discern what would most bless those around her. And, according to her, it's pretty simple— everyone can do it.

But even though Karen describes giving as simple, I know from watching her that her giving often goes beyond comfortable—Karen gives courageously. I have witnessed firsthand as she meets someone's need while having the same need herself. Between the two of us, Karen tends to recognize need first, and because of her we are able to give even when it's a stretch. Without Karen I would miss out on some of these opportunities. She is courageous. She believes. She is brave. I want to be more like her.

Being bravehearted in giving is an attribute of God and is something He is always developing in His people, both the boys who want all the Eggos and the girls who would give you the last one off their plate. He is always inviting us to experience the world through the generosity of His heart. His desire for us is to see and hear the world around us through His eyes and ears. What's really amazing is that as we begin to experience the world this way, we are able to discern the needs and the heart desires of those around us. And we are able to give with authority from the measureless generosity of heaven, which is the same way Jesus gave.

Three Stories

I've been Your echo
I've been Your shadow
But my heart is to know You so I can be Your voice

This promise thing is not about self-fulfillment or good self-esteem. Those are all by-products of embracing the Promise Giver. The core of our promise is really about our Father's purposes on this earth. *"Thy kingdom come...in earth, as it is in heaven"* (Matt. 6:10 KJV). That's what Jesus taught us to pray. You know that's the whole point, right?

God's plan for earth is to see His Kingdom established here, where we live right now. And here's where it gets really cool. He has purposed to use *us* to establish it. He chooses us! He dreams of a marriage, a friendship, a partnership with us in order to establish His Kingdom of heaven on earth. He desires to work His purpose through our promise, and that revelation makes me smile.

Below are three stories of God encounters—three different situations over the years where my Father revealed His heart to me in a profound manner. These three experiences have developed in me the heart of my Father for the world in which I live. From these encounters I've seen His purpose is so much bigger than me, and yet He has amazingly given me a promise that coincides with His purpose, and He wants to partner with me in fulfilling it. These are stories of my heart growing braver.

Story 1: Pandemonium

At the age of eighteen, I had one of the coolest jobs ever. I was a roadie for a successful musician whose name was Phil Driscoll. In the world of the trumpet, he is a god—little *g* of course. He is a trumpet genius. I love the trumpet the way Bon Iver, Radiohead, or The National loves the trumpet, which is to say in small subdued or frenzied symphonic doses. But when Phil plays, he changes my mind. He is a soulful rocker, a supremely talented musician. He is also a man who loves God. I spent six months as a roadie for his ministry, and even though he called me Scott for the first three months, I enjoyed working for him.

I spent most of my days on the road with Dave, Phil's semitruck driver. Dave was a big man. And when I say big, I mean bodyguard for Hulk Hogan big. He was also covered in tattoos, most of them from before he was saved, so they were a little intimidating and at least PG13. Dave introduced me to truck stops, the trucker code, and steak and eggs for breakfast. All three are wonderfully fascinating and could each be the subject of an entire book. On this particular day, though, Dave was sleeping in the truck while the crew who had flown in on Phil's airplane and I set up for a rather unique Atlanta gig.

A typical Phil concert was held in a church. The audience would be anywhere from 1,000 to 10,000, depending on the size of the church. There was a simple rig for the light show, a few keyboards, several trumpets, and a mic. The concert would begin with Phil singing to a sound track, his Joe Cocker voice growling out a hymn. Then at just the right moment, he would grab one of the trumpets on stage and begin to play. And when he plays, God smiles.

This venue, however, was a coliseum in the heart of Atlanta that held about 2,500 people. I can't fully remember the context of the event, but all I know is three inner-city rival schools were crowded into one place to hear the concert. It was very patriotic and had something to do with celebrating freedom and unity.

Did I mention there were three *rival* schools packed into one place? Did I mention we were celebrating unity?

I had traveled most the night to get there, and my job was to setup and help run the light show. I can't remember who all the speakers were, but I think there was a mayor, a few athletes—one was a gold medalist in the previous Atlanta Olympics—and Phil, who was there to provide the patriotic tunes.

The setup was typical with a stage, small light show (red, white, and blue for this occasion), and mics. The trumpets were put out, the keyboards in place. But when it came to the sound booth located in the middle of the seating area, I noticed something was different. There was a chain link fence set up around the sound-board with a door and roof and everything. I didn't think much about it. I assumed it was to protect the gear from getting stolen or vandalized.

We finished the setup, and about an hour later the buses began to arrive and in came the students. One school body was seated on the right side of the coliseum, one school body on the left, and one more in the balcony. The show began with red, white, and blue lights flashing and Phil hitting the high notes on his trumpet. Then the gold medalist began to speak, but at this point I noticed what was going on in the coliseum around me was louder than what was coming from the stage. The students had stopped listening and started yelling at each other.

Suddenly a fight broke out toward the front. I had never seen anything so violent. Immediately a sea of students surged to that spot. I watched a security guard rush over to break it up and he just disappeared in a mass of bodies as they turned on him and began to beat him. I thought someone should help him or at least go wake up Dave the truck driver.

I started for the exit of our little fenced island but was headed off by Robert, Phil's soundman. "There is nothing we can do!" he yelled, and he was right. The first fight was like a match to gasoline. As I looked around, chaos had broken out all over the coliseum. There were fights everywhere. I stood in stunned disbelief as a boy was thrown from the balcony into the sea of people below. People were screaming. Pandemonium.

Eventually the police arrived and began to sweep from the stage, pushing the crowd out of the coliseum through the back exits. Once they had passed our little stockade, I opened the door and followed. I remember Robert telling me I should stay with them, but I wanted to see what was going on. As we got close to the doors, we heard gunshots in the lobby. People began screaming and Robert pulled me against the doorframe as a mass of bodies overpowered the police in terror and came stampeding back into the coliseum.

When it was all over, I remember walking out into the lobby and seeing kids sitting on the ground or leaning against the walls crying. There was blood on the ground in several places, and I specifically remember one girl vomiting in the corner while she wept hysterically.

Apparently the gunshots were from a policemen's gun. He had been overpowered by the mob and his gun had been forcibly taken from him. In the end, no one was killed, although there were several injuries.

CNN showed up in force with helicopters and vans. They interviewed us. And then it was over. It was time to move on. We headed back into the coliseum to tear down the stage just as Dave showed up, rubbing his eyes—"How'd it go?"

I had begun praying at the very beginning of the incident and continued to pray throughout the teardown. In the midst of cranking down the light rack, I felt my Father's presence on me, then He revealed His heart to me, and what I experienced overwhelmed me. I saw past the violence and excitement of the situation. I believe I saw it as my Father saw it. And His heart was broken over the plight of the students, over the hopelessness they felt, the fear and anger and insecurity they knew on a daily basis. And my heart ached with His and it was impossible not to be moved to tears.

I began to weep. At first I tried to contain myself. I was embarrassed—I thought the guys would think I was crying because I was scared. But I couldn't physically contain the tears, and eventually I openly wept as we worked.

Story 2: Lord, Give Me Your Heart

Several years later I was in a prayer meeting. We were crying out for God to reveal His heart to us. During that prayer time, the presence of God fell on me in such a real way that I couldn't move. His holiness was so thick I could hardly breathe. I began to pray out in hunger for more of His presence, for a greater revelation of who He is. At some point, the meeting ended and everyone left except me. But I didn't notice anyone was gone.

For hours I wrestled in prayer with God. I wanted more, a greater encounter, a grander knowing. I was hungry for His presence, not just theory or principles, but the manifest goodness of God that can be seen and experienced, the presence of God we read about in the Book of Acts when the Holy Spirit fell in power.

I wanted to know His heart. My prayer was, "Father, I will not let You go until You bless me. Give me Your heart." It's a legal prayer. Jacob prayed it while holding onto God with fierce determination (see Gen. 32:26).

Suddenly His holiness became manifest. That is to say, I was reverently and fearfully aware of His presence. I heard my Father's voice in my heart. He said, "If I reveal My heart to you in greater measure, I will hold you to greater accountability regarding what I have shown you. Are you sure you want this?"

This question held a profoundly serious tone. I had a moment of sober consideration. But my heart is designed to know Him more—and so is yours—so I said, "Yes, Father, give me Your heart."

What happened next surprised and shocked me to my core. I don't know what I had expected, but it wasn't this. God opened His heart so I could know it, and immediately I felt excruciating emotional pain as I began to realize how He agonized with the lost, the sick, and the hurting. I wept the tears of my Father for the abused and the helpless, for those bound by unbelief. I was overwhelmed with the hell that is daily experienced within our world. And I realized He felt it all. He carried it all. He knew it intimately. I also realized my Father was only showing me the smallest sliver of His pain, but that small revelation was nearly killing me.

Just when I thought I would die of sadness, God began to minister His love to me. His love was greater than the pain and greater than the unbelief—His love was my salvation. At the time I didn't understand why He showed me His heart in the way He did, but I can tell you in hindsight, my heart became pregnant with promise that night.

For several weeks after, if I began to think about that moment, I would break down and cry. I would find myself embarrassed by my tears, but I couldn't seem to stem them. The heart of my Father for His people ravaged me with love.

Story 3: Astrida

For many years we sponsored three kids through the World Vision organization. Karen had a really cool idea of finding three kids who shared the same birth dates as our kids. It was a fun way to make them a part of our lives and include our kids in praying for them and remembering them. Their pictures are still on our fridge to this day.

There was Carmalena—she is Maddy's age and is from Guatemala. Grover is Ethan's age and from Bolivia, and Astrida is from Zambia for Eva Blaze. We sent a small amount each month to help their families in providing for their kids. We would often pray for them at the supper table or before bedtime.

Though we never met these kids or their families, we occasionally received pictures, letters, and information about how they were doing. We received a phone call one day that broke our hearts. Astrida, our youngest, had died.

There was not a clean source for water in her village. Her family had to travel several miles to the next village just to get water. Astrida drank some bad water, got sick, and couldn't keep anything down. She died of dehydration—for lack of clean water.

Karen called to tell me the news. She was obviously emotional. It was hard to believe. There had been no warning, and honestly we didn't even know Astrida's village didn't have clean water until after her death.

Several days after hearing the news, I was sitting in a coffee shop writing this book when my dad stopped in. We discussed our family business for a while, and then I began to tell him about Astrida. I barely started the story before I was crying. And for weeks afterward I couldn't tell the story of Astrida without crying. I am no longer concerned with the tears because I have come to know this is a true expression of the heart of my Father. His heart is broken with the brokenness of this world.

Giving from the Promise

Come, oh Glory, fill my heart, come, oh Brilliance, fill my sight
Every particle of me till I'm a portrait of Your grace

We live in a world that thirsts for the knowledge of God, aches for the presence of true friendship, longs for the love of a Father, and yearns for the hope of a Savior. We live in a world desperate in need—physically, spiritually, and emotionally. You don't have to look hard to see it.

Our Father knows and cares for all our needs. His heart is to meet every one in the power and authority of His love. And I believe it is our Father's desire to partner with us in order to meet those needs. Jesus showed us what that looks like and promised that we could join Him in a life of such powerful generosity. God has invited us to chase Him, to trust Him, and to grow in revelation until we want what He wants, see what He sees, hear what He hears, and go where He goes. He *wants* to give us His heart.

God's heart is for the broken, the lost, the oppressed, the sick, the widow, and the orphan. And He desires to have us bring wholeness to the broken, freedom to the oppressed, and healing to the sick. He has called us to father and mother the orphan and bless the widow. The untamed lifestyle is learning how to give out of our promise, because our promise isn't just for us, it's for the world we live in.

An untamed life is the one where God's priorities become our priorities. What's amazing is when we respond to a God-revealed need, we act within the authority of our promise. I believe a revelation of who He is releases in us the authority to act in who we are. That is to say, who we are is now partnered with who He is in order to meet the need that exists. When that partnership takes place, the impact is not just temporary, it's eternal; it's not just natural, it's supernatural. It's called "Thy Kingdom come."

Often I have responded to need out of sympathy or empathy. And while these can be good motivations for giving, I am learning when I act within the authority and power of God's generosity, the impact is not just good, it's miraculously and infinitely good. The revealed heart of our Father has an answer to every issue in humanity.

Jesus gave generously in the authority of His promise and it often looked miraculous. When there was little food He gave generously, in power and authority, by multiplying it. When there was sickness He gave generously, in power and authority, by healing the person. When there was sin He gave generously, in power and authority, by forgiving it. There is a generosity discovered in the Promise Giver that gives us power and authority to miraculously meet the need.

I am not an expert, but by faith I am finding my way. I am absolutely positive that what Jesus experienced is available to us today.

"Greater works," He said. Can you imagine a generosity that looks like greater works?

As we embrace our promise, a life of trust, a life of radical giving, we will begin to see with greater revelation the heart of our Father for the broken world around us. And not only will our eyes become opened, but our hearts will become moved to engage the need, and our actions will have power and authority. I believe this kind of generous living will change the world.

The Authority of Love

Let Your love be all I know
Till Your glory becomes my own

Years ago I had the privilege to experience how simple generosity given in the power and authority of my promise can change a life. While on a run, I came across a girl who was standing on the sidewalk. She was in her early twenties, and she was limping. I could tell she was distressed. I stopped and asked if she was okay. She had just fallen, and she thought her toe was broken. She was in town visiting her mother, who was at work at the time with the only vehicle. She needed a hospital but didn't know anyone or have transportation to get there.

She was barefoot and I could see the toe was red and swollen. "Can I pray for your toe?" I asked. She seemed a little hesitant but said, "Yes." I prayed, "God, thank You that You love us. I ask for this toe to be made whole right now, in Jesus's name."

Her toe wasn't healed.

I have witnessed people healed of much crazier things than a broken toe. From sprained wrists and ankles to arthritis and sciatica. From cancer defeated, to babies born when doctors said otherwise. I have seen broken marriages redeemed and addictions destroyed. I have seen radical salvations and crazy financial breakthroughs.

Jesus had a 100 percent success rate when He prayed for healing. I am not even close yet, but He said greater works, so I am learning to live and lean into what He promised. I am learning to not allow the times when the miracle doesn't happen to determine how I will believe the next time. If I am going to discover the fullness of my promise I can't afford to allow disappointing experiences to dictate how and what I believe.

So without getting discouraged that her toe wasn't healed when I prayed, I told her I could take her to the emergency room. I asked her to wait at the coffee shop, which was directly across the street, while I ran home to get the minivan. As I ran, I prayed again that God would heal her toe. While I quickly showered and changed, I repeated my prayer for healing. But before I left the house, I had to make a decision.

You see, we only had about $200 in the bank. That money was meant to last the rest of the month and we were only halfway through the month. But I had a feeling this girl didn't have any money. As I walked out the door, I looked at Karen and said, "Babe, I believe it's in God's heart to heal her toe but if..." Before I could finish what I was going to say, Karen responded with, "Yes, we will pay for it." With that question settled in our hearts, I headed to the coffee shop.

When I arrived she was still in pain, her toe still inflamed. As I was helping her into the minivan, she told me she didn't have insurance and didn't know if Medicaid covered her. I told her not to worry. As we drove to urgent care she asked, "Why are you doing this, you don't even know me?" I responded, "Because God loves me, He loves you, and I love you."

When we arrived at urgent care, she signed in and she was correct, they didn't have her in the system. I had been standing beside her at the counter and I stepped in and said, "I've got it." At this point she started crying. They immediately took her into another room. I waited. It wasn't long before she came out with her foot in a protective brace.

On the way back to her house she told me her story. It was a rough one. She had been a drug addict, had been married and then left with her two boys. She had been betrayed and used and unloved. Her life was a mess. As we sat in the minivan outside her house, she again asked, "Why would you do something like this?" I told her the same thing: "Because God loves me, He loves you, and I love you."

She began to cry again, and then she asked a beautiful question: "How do you know that God loves you? How do you know He loves me?" That's when I had the incredible honor of introducing her to Love.

"God is love," I said, "so to know love, you simply say yes to God." She did. Right there in my minivan. While we prayed, God loved her best and she was overwhelmed by His goodness—she experienced His personal one-of-a-kind love for her and was saved.

The greatest miracle on the planet is salvation. In salvation is every other miracle, every other revelation. Jesus came to seek and save that which was lost. Salvation is the invitation to be redeemed, restored, and healed. And it includes every part of us— emotional, physical, and spiritual. This girl encountered Love and was saved. It was a miracle. Just like those Jesus performed.

I am learning how to love, how to see others, and how to act within the generous authority and power of love. This girl's life is forever changed because you can't encounter God's always-good love and not change. It's God's kindness that leads to repentance.

Not once did I manipulate her with my actions. Love isn't like that. She never knew we used the last of our money for her toe. I chose to simply love her and reveal the goodness of God in the process. I was blessed and honored to pray for healing, I was blessed and honored to take her to urgent care, and I would have been blessed and honored even if she didn't ask the question that led to her salvation. My promise is way bigger than getting someone to say a prayer. It is about living powerfully generous—bravehearted.

It was generous love that opened the door to transformation. And now this girl knows she is loved. And isn't that why we are all here, to know we are loved and then love in return? We have been given a promise to establish a legacy of the love of God. This legacy of love is what advances God's heavenly Kingdom even long after we have headed home. How awesome is that?

Pick a Fight

I pledged my head to a holy love,
put down my paper, picked up my guns
We took the hill, me and the thunder sons,
we didn't quit till Thy Kingdom comes

I love the movie *Braveheart*. I remember the first time I saw the preview at a theater. I was with Karen at some *other* movie. I actually can't remember the movie we went to see, as it paled in comparison with the *Braveheart* trailer. I kept telling Karen that I wished the movie we were watching was *Braveheart* until she finally asked me nicely to shut up. I saw it eleven times in the theater. So now you know, as if you didn't by now, I'm a bit odd. That being said, I'm about to go *Braveheart* on you. Ready?

> **Malcolm Wallace to his son:** *Your heart is free. Have the courage to follow it.*

Jesus isn't a long-haired hippie giving us the peace sign. He isn't a shy, granola-eating man who sits quietly in the corner, espousing vagaries on love no more profound than an after-school special, a soft man with a title. He is not powerless or fragile. And neither are we.

We have been sleeping, but we are now waking up. We are the church and there is available to us a righteous anger that will not tolerate injustice, that won't abide oppression. When we see darkness, we must act. We are sure in love and bold in faith, we are *salt and light*—we are believers.

> **William Wallace:** *Go back to England and tell them there that Scotland's daughters and sons are yours no more. Tell them Scotland is free.*

The boy born to be king was furious. David wasn't slightly annoyed—he was mad. "Who is this uncircumcised Philistine that he should defy the armies of the living God?" It is important to know David didn't just kill Goliath out of a desire for advancement. He didn't just take the giant on out of obedience. Goliath actually offended him. He was disgusted with the very idea of Goliath.

Listen to how he speaks to Goliath when he finally gets out on the field of battle:

> *This day the Lord will hand you over to me, and I'll strike you down and cut off your head. Today I will give the carcasses of the Philistine army to the birds of the air and the beasts of the earth, and the whole world will know that there is a God in Israel* (1 Samuel 17:46).

David was raging mad. He saw evil embodied and couldn't stomach the idea of it being allowed to continue breathing. He saw injustice in the flesh and determined to destroy it.

> **William Wallace:** *Men don't follow titles, they follow courage.*

God *is* love. And He's not powerless love. That stuff inspires nothing and it's not what we signed up for. God's love has the power to answer every question humankind is asking. If we truly know Him as love, we will know He is the most powerful force that has ever existed.

God stands before us and says, "Every man dies, but not every man truly loves." I told you I was going *Braveheart* on you. Yes, I changed that last word. I changed it because I believe to love is to live and anything less is death. Either death now or death later—it really doesn't matter because death is death. But love? Love is life abundant and sets us powerfully free.

> **William Wallace:** *Free men you are. What will you do with that freedom?*

Our family, our neighborhood, our country, and our world are waiting for believers to act with true revelation from the heart of Love. They are waiting for us to give out of our partnership with God, in the power and authority of our promise. They are waiting for us to get righteously raging mad, maybe even pick a fight. They are waiting for us to say to injustice and intolerance and hatefulness and unrighteousness and poverty and disease and abuse and hunger: "Enough is enough! How dare you defy the armies of the living God!"

The promise of a greater works life, the salvation of our families, our country, and our world is not in the hands of politicians or even our culture's Christian leaders. It's in the hands of a church that has awakened to their promise—to the power and authority of generous love. It's in the hands of surrendered and untamed believers—brave-hearted sons and daughters.

> **William Wallace/Jason Clark:** *Stay safe and you'll live… at least awhile. And dying in your beds, many years from now, or maybe in your churches months from now, would you be willing to trade all your safety, from this day to that, for one chance—just one chance—to stand and tell the giant that he may take our lives, but he'll never take our LOVE!*

Father God is awakening us to His love and we are discovering that we are giant killers, it's what our promise looks like—it's our birthright, our destiny. My prayer is that God would stretch our hearts to give and quench our righteous anger through radical acts of love, that we would know His presence, and from that relationship live the miraculous greater works life He has promised all of us. The world is waiting for it—we owe them an encounter with His love.

That's what going *Braveheart* looks like. I hope that put some wind under your kilt.

Calling All Bravehearts

I put down my paper, picked up my guns
We took the hill, me and the Thunder Sons

I am learning how to share my Eggos—Ethan too. I am learning how to live for my kids, my family, my neighbors, and even this world. I am learning to be bravehearted, like Karen. I want to live powerfully generous, with my time and our finances. I want to be found faithful. And I want to leave that legacy to my kids as well.

Bravehearted giving is how we battle against the evils of this world. Partnering with God and giving from our promise is the most powerful thing we will ever do with our lives. It's time for you and me, the church, to put aside our safe, long-haired-hippie version of Jesus, the One with powerless love, and embrace the Man who gave His very life. Giving is what sets people free. Giving is what saved the world. Jesus has invited us to join Him.

Generous giving is our birthright. It's a partnership with our Father's heart. It always further aligns our affections with His. I am learning how to live powerfully through daily and monthly decisions to give. And I would encourage you today to find a place to give as well.

Karen and I continue to support organizations like World Vision. One of the desires of my family is to give in the area of clean water, especially in Zambia. If you would like to partner with my family regarding clean water, you can go to World Hope's website. Both

World Hope and World Vision have wonderful child sponsorship programs. Visit www.worldhope.org or www.worldvision.org today. Find what tugs on your heart, your giant, and then be intentional about giving toward that. It's a great place to start.

Chapter 13

Let's Go Find This Kingdom Come

Practiced in His Presence

I turn my face to a blazing sun
Your glory falls, Your Kingdom comes

I was in my mid-twenties leading worship on a Sunday morning the day the church had a guest speaker I highly respected. When I lead worship, most of the time my eyes are closed, so I didn't see the speaker come on the stage and stand next to me. He gently touched my arm. He had a microphone and looked like he wanted to share. I brought the song to a close. At first, I thought he would have a word from God for the church, but as he spoke I realized he was talking to me.

"I would like you to take your guitar and step down off the stage," he said kindly. As I followed his instructions, he continued: "Now turn your back to the church, face the front." I complied. "Now worship," he said. I looked at him, a little confused. He smiled reassuringly and said, "Worship like you have been doing all morning but pretend we aren't here. Worship the way you do when you are at home by yourself."

I began to play. At first I was a little uncomfortable—I could feel the people watching, waiting. But I pressed through. I began to praise God in song while playing a random chord progression. I praised Him for His goodness; I thanked Him for His love and for my wife and my new baby girl. At some point I actually forgot about the 200 people behind me. Just like when I am alone in my living room, God's presence became real to me. I worshiped this way for about ten minutes. I forgot the people; it was just God and me. I started to sing a song: "I am standing in Your presence on holy ground."

As I began to sing, the band, who were still onstage, joined in. Then the 200 people behind me joined in. I climbed back onstage as that song led to another and another until we had worshiped forty more minutes or so. It was a sweet time, one of my fondest worship memories.

As we came to a holy stillness, I looked up to see the speaker had joined us again onstage. He looked directly at me and said, "You can only take people where you have already been. If you go first, you will stir those around you to hunger for a greater revelation of God"—a greater love encounter. "You must be practiced in His presence."

Every one of us has a promise that is way bigger than we can imagine. It's a promise that isn't just for us but for the world we live in. This promise isn't found on a stage, it's not about a title; our promise is birthed in the heart of our Father and is encountered in His presence.

God is looking for men and women who are not focused on a stage—those who aren't seeking titles but instead are seeking His presence. We can't take people where we haven't been. We can't give what we don't have. We must be practiced in His presence. We must know how to worship when no one is looking so we can worship where everyone can see.

David killed the bear and the lion while shepherding in obscurity before he killed the giant in a crowd. David experienced and demonstrated who God was while alone in his "living room" before he ever experienced and demonstrated who God was on a national stage. For David, it was never about a stage. It was always about the presence, and because of that he was a king long before he wore the crown.

This world doesn't need more crown-seeking kings, but it's hungry for true kings—sons and daughters who are sure in His love, practiced in His presence, living sure in their promise, pulling His Kingdom to earth.

So-and-So *and* So What!

I believe in revolution,
Love's not an institution

A friend of mine was starting a church and asked me to come and lead worship for the group that was meeting in his home. I arrived early so I could hang out before starting the service, and also for the cookies. One of the fellas went awkwardly out of his way to introduce himself as a former pastor.

When it was my turn, I told him I moved a lot as a kid, living in several states and provinces. Often in introductions, when I tell people my history, the next question is, "Was your dad in the armed forces?" When asked this question, I almost always respond, "Yes, he is a pastor." It's easier than saying, "No, he is a pastor," but just barely.

At my answer, the former pastor's eyes grew wide with knowing. "Ah yes, so is he still pastoring?" he asked with reverent emphasis on the word *"pastoring."*

"All the time!" I admit it; I was having a little fun.

"Where is his church?" he asked seriously and slightly concerned.

"Mostly spread throughout the Southeast," I responded.

"What's the name of his church?" The confusion on the former pastor's face was clear.

"Let's see, there's the Clark family church, there's the friends church, and the church of the unbelievers—that's one of his favorites—then there's the business church and the neighbors church... well, you get it." I added reverent emphasis on the last phrase, hoping he would get it. But I don't think he did. I think he needed the title of *pastor* more than the title needed him.

Let's say I'm at a picnic and there's fried chicken and corn on the cob, and jalapeno hamburgers infused with sharp cheddar, and maybe some Chipotle Kettle potato chips. Then a genuine someone says, "Jason, let me introduce you to So-and-So," and then So-and-So puts out his hand and, with pomp and ceremony, says, "I'm *Dr.* So-and-So."

I might want to respond with "I'm Singer-Songwriter Jason," or "I'm Author Jason," or "I'm Briefs-over-Boxers Jason." I am not saying I responded that way, I'm just saying that if this had actually happened I might have wanted to. You get it, right? I can wear a lot of titles, but none of them are needed at the picnic. A title is never for the person who has it; a title is always about serving the person who needs it.

Let's change the scenario a little bit. I've had a triple black accident or something. My right arm has fallen off, there's some blood, and it's not good. So I'm walking around the hospital with a detached right arm clutched in my left hand when I'm introduced to Hank. My first question for Hank is, "Are you Dr. Hank?" If Hank says, "No, I'm Janitor Hank," then Hank is not the fella I'm looking for. While janitor Hank is important, sorry about the mess Hank, right now I really need *Dr.* So-and-So.

We absolutely love titles in our culture. And we really love them in our churches. We spend big bucks and years earning them. And it's not a bad system, at least for this world. But it's not how God's Kingdom works—and His Kingdom is coming. Trust me, it's coming. In our Father's eyes we are defined only by our relationship with Jesus and by His thoughts about us.

When the former pastor asked if my dad was a pastor, I said yes. But had he asked if my dad were a business owner, I would have said yes to that as well. If you need a pastor, my dad is your man—he always sees Jesus in people and he lays his life down on their behalf so they would know God more. He is filled with compassion and is bravehearted in his generosity to meet needs. His church is spread across the world and is not confined to the Sunday morning model. However, it's been years since my dad needed to be called *pastor,* and it's been even more years since he had a pulpit, but who needs a pulpit if we know the Father? Not my dad.

We don't need a title to see people like Jesus sees them or tell people how Jesus loves them or serve people in Jesus's name. We certainly don't need ordination papers to love with power and authority. Our Father has already ordained us, called us, set us apart for His glory to be revealed through us. Simply put, we don't need a title to validate or embrace our promise.

In fact, I have seen firsthand that giving people titles when it's not who they truly are not only hurts the body of believers but also the one living under a false title. You can call me *Dr.* So-and-So till you're blue in the face. Lead me to a fella who is missing his right arm, and hand me his right arm and the sewing kit. But in the end we would discover to our horror, and possibly his death, I am just a simple Bible college graduate.

I believe with my whole heart that the calling to be a pastor or teacher as a full-time occupation is wonderful, biblical, and essential (Eph. 4:11–13). I believe the community of believers is God's idea, and like all His ideas it is absolutely stunning. Sunday morning is beautiful, or at least it should be. But please understand me: it's not the full expression of God's Kingdom here on earth. And it certainly isn't what most of our promises look like.

I have met many who believe ministry is something done by professionals—the guys and girls with the titles, the ones who went to seminary. I am telling you ministry is a lifestyle, an untamed faith, a radical trust, a willingness to say yes, to obey. Ministry is our promise and it can't be left just to the handful with titles. Ministry is simply sons and daughters saying yes to their promise. It is the by-product of living loved. And it doesn't need a stage, a podium, a degree, or a title; it simply needs a surrendered heart.

You are the pastor of your neighborhood, the teacher of the good news to your family, the gospel on display at your workplace. You are a minister of the goodness of Jesus. You are His favorite, the one designed to live sure in love. You are the one who is called to bring heaven to earth, the one created to experience miracles, the one He promised would discover a greater works life.

Our Promise Is Our Ministry

I had a dream tonight and You were there
A bride in brilliant white and You were there

When I was in China, I met with an amazing believer. He had moved there thirty years earlier with a vision to share the love of Jesus with the Chinese people. Due to the fact that China is a Communist country, he couldn't live there as a "missionary," nor could he speak too openly about Jesus. So God led him to engage his promise through becoming a businessman.

As we sat and talked one afternoon over eel, chicken heads, and duck feet, among other exquisite entrees I can only begin to guess at, he gave me a truth from his life experience. "Believers are not called to advance the church," he said. "We are called to advance God's Kingdom. Our promise is to establish His Kingdom on earth as it is in heaven." This truth had empowered my business, missionary, chicken-head-eating friend to powerfully release the Kingdom of heaven in China.

In the United States the institutional model of church has traditionally been the vehicle that has advanced God's Kingdom. Not so in China. At least for this man, it has been through his business that he has seen God's Kingdom coming. The truth he shared with me was good, but what made it profound was he had just taken me on a tour of one of his factories, which was home to 400-plus workers, of which 80 percent were believers. This is an amazing percentage in any country, but in China it's beyond amazing. It's truly miraculous.

Then he told me story after story of his employees preaching the gospel to their community, and of the miracles and healings that were taking place in the city where his company is located. He told stories of underground churches being started and strengthened and led by his believing employees. There were even stories of government officials being saved due to the impact his company has had on the city.

Then we saw the awards that had been given to the company. Over the previous nine years his company had consistently won the award for the best place to work in that particular city. He told us of a health plan they had put together for the employees, which is something unheard of in China. On top of that, I had already visited an orphanage, partially funded by the missionary-businessman's company, where I wept joyfully to see special needs children loved and cared for.

In China, the government has restricted couples to one child. Therefore, if a child is born with medical issues, it is not unusual for them to be abandoned. These babies, if they are found and survive, are given to the state and then grow up with very little human contact or interaction. They live unloved in an institution bed. I heard horror stories of how they are treated, stories that would both break your heart and make you furious.

But I had witnessed an orphanage where "undercover" believers have been invited to come in and partner with the state. I had the opportunity to see the results: beautiful kids, eyes bright, laughing and learning—one worker per child, which was another miracle. The workers there were radically in love with God; it was evident in how they loved the children.

Now, get this: not only is this company profoundly changing their city and their nation, the company is also profitable. That was important. My missionary-business friend went out of his way to highlight that fact. Why? Because a business that is not profitable is also a business that is not successful. The Kingdom isn't limited to churches, ministries, and nonprofit organizations. Along with everything else, this man's ministry looked like a profit margin. God's idea of heaven on earth, His heart for ministry, includes profit margins.

This truth impacted me greatly because it put words to a frustration that had been growing in me since early adulthood. We live in a country that primarily still believes church is a Sunday morning experience. Even with all the emergent whatever it is, that's still the prevailing view in the good old US of A. But that's not the church deep and wide. The church is you and me advancing God's Kingdom through our promises, our giftings, our abilities, and our graces. It should look like homes filled with wonder, workplaces filled with hope, universities, parks, grocery stores, hospitals, and church services filled with love. It should look this way because we are there, and we are growing sure in His love—we are a living ministry.

Please get this. Our promise doesn't have to fit within the context of Sunday morning to be validated as ministry. Our promise *is* our ministry, and every one of us has one. Regardless of a title, we are all ministers. Our promises are no less profound or relevant if they land us outside of a full-time position at a church. We came into relationship with God to know Him, be transformed, and advance His Kingdom through our promise. It should look as varied and unique as the hand is to the nose, is to the hip, is to the eye. We are one body, one church, and no two of us are the same.

Swimming against the Stream

Let's go find this Kingdom come, well done

When I was five years old, my dad and mom were asked by my kindergarten teacher to come in to discuss my behavior. Now, I can't remember much from kindergarten. There were the monkey-bar fights, where two boys hung from the bars by their hands and tried to wrap their legs around the other's torso in order to yank them off the bars.

I remember "smash-up derby," where all us boys would put our arms down at our sides and then run at each other as fast as we could, trying to knock each other down while making car noises. And I remember hanging from my jeans belt loop off the top of the swing set pretending I was superman and I could fly. Eventually the belt loops would tear. The last time I played that game, I wasn't quick enough to grab the bar, and the fall resulted in getting the wind knocked out of me. I remember that. And I remember my mom wondering aloud in an annoyed manner why my belt loops kept tearing. And I remember not having a clue. Stupid jeans.

But apparently along with all my painful landings, I was quite the preacher as well. It seems I didn't want my classmates living in blind ignorance. I felt it was important they knew Jesus was real and Santa Claus wasn't. Yes, I was *that* kid. And apparently my teacher thought it was the other way around, which is why he called my parents in.

The teacher told my parents I was "very different" from the other kids in that I spoke about God as if I knew Him, as if *He* were real. He said it was causing me to stand out, and then he used an analogy that has defined me most of my life: I was "swimming against the stream."

My beautiful father responded, "Yes, that's exactly what he is doing and I pray he never quits." My dad spoke that over my life when I was just five years old. Looking back, it truly was prophetic. It has been one of the determining characteristics molding me into who I am today. For most of my adult life, I have found myself swimming not just against a worldly current but also often counter to "religious culture."

Reformation

Love's not an institution

By the time I finished Bible college, I'd had my fill of institution. It wasn't the college, because it's a wonderful school and God led me there. I felt called to ministry but I couldn't make the clothes of a pastor or worship leader or missionary fit. And at the time, those seemed to be my only options. It was kind of like David trying to wear Saul's armor. The titles chafed.

So instead of "Pastor Jason," I continued my five-year-old destiny—swimming against the stream. I had begun dreaming of Jesus and rock 'n' roll, and soon I was in a band. I remember the night we named it. My bandmates, our wives, and I sat around the kitchen table, and over empty spaghetti plates we began discussing possible names for our newly formed group. "Fringe" was one of the first offerings and in the end the name I thought fit best. At the time, I truly felt like I was a member of the fringe, especially in regard to the church I knew.

Our first studio album was titled *For the Vagabond Believer.* Looking back, that's what we were—vagabonds, homeless wanderers walking through our small piece of the world, telling the truth to any who would listen. Though it sounds romantic, it was actually quite lonely. Kind of like swimming upstream.

Those years on the fringe formed me. I learned to believe and trust. I grew more sure in an always-good God. I began to understand my promise or my *ministry calling* wasn't about expanding an institutional model of church, but about becoming the church sure in love that expands His Kingdom.

As I have begun to see in the much larger context of the Kingdom, I have discovered my God is not a fringe God, He is right at the center of things. In fact, He *is* the center. In these last years I have learned my promise isn't about leaving a culture but reforming it, creating it, defining it. That promise isn't unique to me—it's the call of every believer.

Do you know what's funny? Over the last several years I have worn the title of pastor. That's right. The kid who once couldn't make the suit fit discovered it was his understanding regarding the suit that didn't fit. The kid who was once leery of titles has discovered he can wear one. You see, our promises have nothing to do with the title pastor or doctor or plumber or schoolteacher; our promises have everything to do with His promise "Thy Kingdom come."

I no longer desire to be on the fringe, yet neither will I try to fit a mold. I've come to see there's swimming against the stream just to swim against the stream, and then there's swimming against the stream like the salmon do—to give life so others might live and to get back home. You face predators along the way, you're misunderstood, the trip is exhausting, and you die a thousand deaths, but you do it for the glory and the story.

Along the way I have met many other vagabond believers, untamed fools who, like myself, have been redefining the paradigm of what ministry looks like. We are learning it's never about a stage or a title, but it is always about discovering His presence, His good love. It's never been about how the suit fits, it's always been about faith, hope, and love. We have grabbed hold of our promise to release the Kingdom of God into the world.

You and I are the church. Sunday morning services are only one way to swim. God desires the Kingdom to break into education, the arts and entertainment, and our government. He wants Kingdom-minded businessmen, and so on. God longs for a church deep and wide.

> I'm an artist who is a Christian. I'm not a Christian artist.
>
> —JOHNNY CASH

There is no such thing as Christian music; there are only musicians who believe. There is no such thing as Christian books; there are only writers who believe. There is no such thing as Christian businesses; there are only businessmen who believe. There is no such thing as Christian education; there are only teachers who believe.

It is time for the church to swim against the stream in all of our promised glory. We were not meant to live on the fringe. We are not meant to run from or build a Christian subculture. We were never meant to hide out and wait for the King's return. We are born to colabor with Him and create the world He will return to. We are called to reformation until the love of God is revealed through His church, and the world is transformed. Sure, there are days when that is hard to believe, but we've got to remember that things are not what they seem.

We Are the Giants

As a sacred sky descends,
Hey friends, it's time we got going

When David stepped out on the battlefield, the people's perception was not reality. To the onlookers, it appeared that David was just a foolish boy, small and weak in comparison to Goliath. But David perceived a greater reality—God's reality. It is a reality that is unseen, one that is to be lived by faith. And in God's story, we are the giants. We have already won.

It's time we began to agree with a higher reality, a greater truth. This world is ours. We are the giants. It may not look like it at times, and it may not feel like it, but it is the truth. The Bible says, *"The One who is in you is greater than the one who is in the world"* (1 John 4:4). There is a way of living that risks it all on the revelation that God has given us the land to take, that darkness is no more when light shines.

I'm convinced God is looking for surrendered sons and daughters, untamed believers who know Him, trust Him, obey Him, and then risk everything to bring heaven to earth—those who are practiced in His presence. We can be the worshipers who make breakthrough available for everyone else. David's victory was all of Israel's victory.

Romans 8:19 says, *"The creation waits in eager expectation for the sons of God to be revealed."* The sons of God? Yes, you got it—that's us! We are the giants. When we begin to walk in a revelation of the overwhelming love of Christ Jesus, we begin to embrace the power and authority He died to give us. Paul goes on to assure us, *"If God is for us, who can be against us? He who did not spare His own Son, but gave Him up for us all—how will He not also, along with Him, graciously give us all things?"* (Rom. 8:31-32).

God's love is the most powerful thing in the world, and it's also the most beautiful. Its power is displayed in Jesus's resurrection, and its beauty is revealed in the lives of those who journey with Him. We have access to a heavenly truth we have only begun to understand. We have barely scratched the surface of our glorious promise. I am absolutely convinced we have not yet seen on earth the full wonders of God's love.

It's time to live untamed. It's time to wake the sleeping giant within. It's time to believe and experience signs and wonders. It's time to believe His promises and run headlong into a greater works life. May the church deep and wide continue to say yes to an untamed faith, and may the world be changed because of it.

Let's go find this Kingdom come.

About Jason Clark

JASON CLARK is an author, speaker, singer/songwriter and director of *A Family Story*. Jason's passion is to discover and grow sure in the always-good love of our heavenly Father; His mission is to tell the story so sons and daughters may grow sure.

He and his wife, Karen, live in North Carolina with their three children.

For more information on Jason's books or albums, go to www.jasonclarkis.com.

About A Family Story

Over the last several years I have had the honor of connecting with the church deep and wide. I have shared in the story of our Father's love at home and in my travels. I am convinced His story is ours as well. It's a family story and the only one He is telling.

A Family Story is a relational community of creatives—my family and friends. We do life together; we envision and express God's love through our giftings and grace. We are a tribe of worshippers, dreamers, storytellers, and preachers; a family of moms and dads, brothers and sisters, daughters and sons, united by our singular passion—to know and reveal God's perfect love.

Our online home is www.afamilystory.org, where we can share what God is revealing through the lives of family and friends. There are some amazing books, albums, films, messages, and articles on this site, resources that will greatly encourage you as you journey into our Father's always-good love.

For more information on the community and ministry of my family and friends, you can go to www.afamilystory.org.

Many of the song lyrics featured in this book, *Untamed*, are from Jason Clark albums, *Heaven's Crush* and *Surrendered & Untamed*.

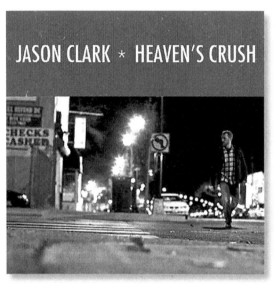

Both albums are available at
www.jasonclarkis.com

Praise for Jason's latest albums:

"*Heaven's Crush* is a spacious beautiful addition to Clark's catalog. It's the kind of music that brings the chaos of life into focus. If you are looking for music that will move your soul, then *Heaven's Crush* is for you."

—MARK FISHER

"Both lyrically and instrumentally, Jason is wildly creative and builds an atmosphere of awe that lends itself to sincere worship... *Surrendered & Untamed* will lead you as far into the presence as you are willing to go."

—KEVAN BREITINGE

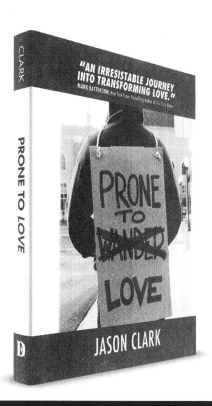

STOP TRYING TO BECOME WHO YOU ALREADY ARE!

What if we actually lived out of the relationship and reality we talked, preached, and sung about?

We would change the world.

The roadblock preventing us from stepping into our identities as sons and daughters of God is **not** lack of discipline, resources, or creative ideas. We have all of this…

What's missing? To discover who you are, first, you must know Who the Father is and what He's like.

JOIN *the* CLUB

As a member of the **Love to Read Club,** receive exclusive offers for FREE, 99¢ and $1.99 e-books* every week. Plus, get the **latest news** about upcoming releases from **top authors** like...

T.D. Jakes, Bill Johnson, Cindy Trimm, Jim Stovall, Beni Johnson, Myles Munroe, *and more!*

JOIN NOW at *destinyimage.com/freebooks*

SHARE *this* BOOK

Don't let the impact of this book end with you! **Get a discount when you order 3 or more books.**

CALL TO ORDER
1-888-987-7033

destinyimage.com  1-800-722-6774

34363527R00134

Printed in Great Britain
by Amazon